A Journey Thro'
My Childhood

Marion
Darby

A Journey Thro' My Childhood

Malcolm Darby

The Pentland Press Limited
Edinburgh • Cambridge • Durham • USA

First published in 1994 by
Arkleside Publications

This edition published in 1996 by
The Pentland Press Ltd.
1 Hutton Close
South Church
Bishop Auckland
Durham

British Library Cataloguing in Publication Data.
A Catalogue record for this book is available
from the British Library.

ISBN 1 85821 368 1

Typeset by CBS, Felixstowe, Suffolk
Printed and bound by Antony Rowe Ltd., Chippenham

My father was a coal miner.
The book is dedicated to
him and every coal miner
of his generation.

CONTENTS

PREFACE

In this age of television, video, music centres and computers etc. it must be difficult for the youngsters of today to imagine a life without them or how to fill their spare time.

The things that we today take for granted as the absolute essentials of life, such as the car, the telephone, the bath, central heating, were all items of sheer luxury and were only within the reach of the well-off when I was a child.

As a person who is fortunate to own all or most of the luxuries of life that I require, I can honestly say that anyone who cannot enjoy these things does not know what they are missing. Those who are no longer with us and who departed this life before today's mechanical and technological joys were even thought of, were indeed unfortunate not to be part of this wondrous and luxurious life.

I consider however that today's children are missing much more of life by having those electrical gadgets and toys for family and self amusement. In my opinion the reason why there is so much vandalism, brutality and hooliganism is because the kids of today have everything and instead of sharing in the enjoyment of team and group activities or playing simple uncomplicated games, they fight each other in groups and gangs and will yearn for the latest electronic gadget once their current one is out of date.

The vandals and hooligans of today would appear to have absolutely no respect for other people's person or property and in a lot of cases will go very much unpunished, not only by society, if they are indeed caught, but also by their own parents.

In my childhood we certainly were not angels, indeed we were right little devils. The difference was that our 'crimes' were simple and small and more mischievous than destructive. The reason was that our childhoods were relatively simple and most people didn't have much and didn't have all that much for you not to respect.

More important than this was the fact that a clip round the ear or worse from your dad if you put a foot wrong was incentive enough to be good. Likewise, six of the best from your teacher for misbehaving in class and another thumping from dad when you got home if you told him you'd been caned, put the fear in you. Had I been only a fraction of the like of today's vandals and hooligans I would have been permanently black and blue and would have had permanently thick ears. That, in my opinion, is the difference between the children then and the children of today.

This story covers the life I can remember from the age of two to about thirteen years old. I am writing this book for my own children and for their future children, my grandchildren, with the hope that they will know what they have missed and yet appreciate what they have.

I am also writing it in memory of my own father and mother whose childhoods, I know, would in turn have been horrendous compared to my own and would have had a bearing on the way they brought me up. This they no doubt carried out to the best of their ability, in the way they thought the best and with the resources and finances available. I hope you enjoy my story.

Malcolm Darby

PROLOGUE

BALLAD OF A COAL MINER

Now this is the tale of a miner,
A coal miner rugged and tough,
Who worked long hours underground
In water, mud and stuff.

That miner was my father,
A small man, five foot two,
With muscles like Charles Atlas
A miner through and through.

His hands were big like shovels
And his arm muscles hard and solid
But the rest of his body was little
He was lithe and strong and stolid.

He went down the pit at only fourteen
To start a life of hard toil.
'Tha leavin school,' said his father
'Tha gooin to t'pit to shovel coil.'

He worked long hours for a few bob a week
Whether he liked it or not,
Working in water up to his waist
Covered in dirt, sweat and snot.

Day after day it was always the same
Sweat and toil and hard graft,
No air, no breeze, no sunshine,
Till at last they came up the shaft.

I can picture him now with black face and flat hat,
A titch of a thing, just a lad,
Trudging from t'mine wet and tired
With his work mates and his brothers and dad.

Then when he was eighteen his money went up
And he became a man like his brothers,
Seven there were and a sister anawl
And a father and 'wicked' stepmother.

They lived in a terraced house near to the mine
With a yard and outside latrines,
Six brothers in one bed, three at each end,
They looked like a tin of sardines.

He'd come home from t'pit all covered in dust
With eyes and pink lips showing through
But they didn't have bathrooms in those days
So there were always a right to-do.

They'd to have a bath in front of t'fire
In a zinc bath, one after another,
Six brothers, himself and his father,
And in front of his sister and mother.

Then his mother had to wash eight sets of clothes
All covered in sweat, dust and grime
By hand in a tub with no soap-flakes
There were no washing machines at that time.

But when he grew up mi mam he did meet
And they set up house and got wed
And he left his terrace of squalor
To have his own house instead.

He became a typical miner
A hard-working, hard-drinking fellow,
He'd swear and spit and fart as well
And he could certainly shout and bellow.

He smoked like a chimney, mi father,
Sixty Woodbines a day,
And eight pints of Bitter or Guinness
At the pub just a stone's throw away.

He went to the pit, came home for his grub
Then went to the pub every night,
He'd then come home to sleep it off
Sometimes with mi mam he would fight.

His favourite place was a chair by the fire
No one dared sit in his spot
He could sit there and spit in the fire
Without moving – he was a very good shot.

Now it might sound quite horrid this spitting,
Loathsome and dirty at best,
But how does a hard-working miner
Get rid of the dust off his chest.

I remember dad's face so clearly
All covered in coal dust and grit,
And his hands and nose had black and blue scars
Etched in his skin from the pit.

He worked in the pit some fifty-one years
Through illness and injury too
But I never heard him grumble
There was nowt else he could do.

When the time came for retirement
At the age of sixty-five
I can't help but think and wonder
How he'd managed to survive.

I think of all his smoking
And the drinking that he did
But I also think of all the toil
He did from just a kid.

For twenty years he still sat there
In his chair with Woodbines and such,
Still spitting coal dust into the fire
And still not missing the target much.

But now he's gone at eighty-six
His toil and hard work done,
He had a hard life that's for sure
Which couldn't have been much fun.

And when he came to me to live
A year before he died
He didn't need removal vans
Or tea chests or boxes tied.

Oh no, he had a carrier bag
With everything he had
For fifty years of toil and sweat
By a Yorkshire coal mining lad.

This is how my story-writing all began, thinking about the demise of the
Coal Industry and the heritage of South Yorkshire.

CHAPTER ONE

MY HOUSE

When I were a lad, oh! a long time ago
My life was both horrid and funny;
We didn't have much, no luxuries as such
We certainly didn't have any money.

We lived in a house at Wath in Ash Road,
A terrace with garden and passage,
It didn't belong to mi mam or mi dad
Just a typical Council messuage.

The house had a gate from the passage
A rickety one, home made by dad,
Then a fence between us and our neighbours
Then they had a gate to their pad.

Now our passage wall had a coal hole
With a battered and old wooden door
At high level where dad chucked coal in
That he'd previously tipped on the floor.

He barrowed it down from the pavement
And many's the time I'm sure
That he thought of the back breaking hours
He'd shovelled it from t'mine days before.

Now our coal hole led straight into t'kitchen
With its draught and its muck and its smell,
Where coal and dust fell onto t'lino
And it spread thro' to t'pantry as well.

The house had a 'Room' and a 'Kitchen'
And a small grubby room with a bath
Then an outside porch with a toilet
That led out to the garden path.

The bath was old and decrepit,
The toilet was cold and so glum,
And when you sat out there in winter
Your bum and your legs were quite numb.

The 'Room' had a blazing fire
In winter and summer and fall
With a 'range' where mam did all t'cooking,
Potatoes and puddings anawl.

Mi dad had a chair by t'fire
An ash tray and Woodbines a must,
He would cough and spit on t'fire
To get rid of phlegm and coal dust.

Three bedrooms upstairs with no heating,
In winter you couldn't keep warm
But I had an RAF Greatcoat
On mi bed so I came to no harm.

The Greatcoat were mi brother Ken's cast-off
That he had, cos he were in t'RAF,
And when I think now of it covering mi bed
Ee it makes mi want to laugh.

Many's the time in winter though
It were so cold you wouldn't believe,
I'd have t'Greatcoat buttoned up round mi blankets
And I'd sleep wi mi arms in t'sleeves.

We didn't have a bath or a basin
Or a toilet to go to upstairs
But I had a po under my bed
I could use when I knelt down for prayers.

I can still remember those bedrooms
The cold, the bare lino, the smell
Of dampness and unemptied chambers
And mi Greatcoat-cum-blanket as well.

I had another way to keep warm though,
At least when I got into bed,
I never had a hot-water bottle
I had an oven plate instead.

The Yorkshire Range had an oven
And in it were one or two shelves
Made of a flat sheet of iron or steel
Which I would take from the oven myself.

Now these oven plates were always red-hot
Because the fire was burning all day,
They were also hard and heavy as well
But they'd make mi bed warm where I lay.

I would take a plate out of t'oven
And wrap it in a piece of old cloth
And I'd sneak up to bed with it under mi arm
If mam knew she'd be quite full of wrath.

It was so very cold in mi bedroom
That breath would come out of mi nose,
I could see it in the light of mi candle
And the lino would be cold on mi toes.

It was lovely to get into bed though,
With the hotplate under mi feet
With Greatcoat 'topping' to cover mi up
On top of a flannelette sheet.

There was only one problem with this
That the hotplate became very hard,
So as soon as you got nice and cosy and warm
The hotplate it was time to discard.

So I'd shove the hotplate from the bed
And the edge on the floor would bang,
It would then topple over and crash to the floor
Making a din with its 'clang.'

I'm surprised I didn't wake all t'house up
Cos we'd no carpets to deaden t'sound,
When t'hotplate fell from t'bed on t'lino
But ni mind it's a lovely bed warmer I've found.

Another way to keep warm in bed
Of course is to keep your socks on
Then your feet would be lovely and warm
In any situation.

And when mi mother found out
I was keeping mi socks on in bed,
She made a stupid remark
That at the time filled me with dread.

'Tha shouldn't keep thi socks on in bed
So I just want thi to stop nar and think,
That if tha continues to do it I tell thi right nar
Thi feet'll be so hot they'll shrink.'

I was horrified to think that mi feet would go small,
They were small enough as it was!
And how could I play football if that was the case?
I'll leave them off, mam's boss.

And you know, I believed that for years,
So I never had socks on in bed
It meant that mi feet had to stay cold at night
Or I'd to have an oven plate instead.

There's another thing that caused quite a fuss
It happened on a warm summer night
I got under mi bed to play
And fell asleep all cosy and tight.

At this time I shared t'same room as Ken
And when he came upstairs to bed
He looked on mi bed expecting to see me
But realised he was on his own instead.

'Where's our Malcolm?' he said to our Bet,
'I aint gor a clue where he is.'
They never thought to look under t'bed
And got themselves right in a tizz.

Dad was at work and mam had gone out
And Ken began to get worried.
'If I don't find him quick,' he said to our Bet,
'When they come back I'll be buried.'

They looked all round the house, outside anawl
They even went round to next door,
Then they came back upstairs, looked under t'bed
And saw me asleep on the floor.

Our Ken was never dad's favourite
It's a good job I was tucked up in bed
Cos if dad had got home and found me not there
He'd probably have kicked in Ken's head.

While on the subject of bed
In my case things could have been better
Because amongst other things
Unfortunately I was a bed-wetter.

I can still remember it now,
I dreamt I was going to the loo,
I can feel the warmth of the urine
Wetting mi bed and clothes through.

I can remember it feeling quite warm
Although I was still half asleep,
In the morning I could feel it all wet and cold
As out of my bed I would creep.

I know I did it for quite a few years
And I really felt sorry for mum
Cos she had the bed sheets and 'jamas to wash
It must have been really quite glum.

I can't really think why I did it,
Some say that it's cos you're depressed,
But in my case I didn't want to get out of bed
That must be the reason I guess.

CHAPTER TWO

MY DAD

My dad was a typical miner
Hardworking, hard drinking and tough,
With his Woodbines and Whitworth's Best Bitter
And Guinness and Buffs and stuff.

Since fourteen he had worked as a miner
He'd slaved in the depths of the pit,
He had scars on his hands, his arms and his face
Got from roof falls, sharp edges and grit.

He suffered from ulcers and ruptures
And yet he would never complain,
He'd just sit there holding his stomach
You knew he was suffering some pain.

A small man was my father
Standing only five foot two,
But he worked hard for his family
And worked hard for himself too.

He had a voice like thunder
And boy, when he was cross,
He'd shout and bawl but never hit
You always knew who were boss.

The Oak Tree Inn was his main haunt
His dominoes, Buffs and beer,
It's all he lived for really
His nights were all spent there.

There was one consolation however
Of his phobia with the pub,
And that was membership of the Oak Tree Inn
Barnsley Supporters' Club.

We would board our coach on Saturdays
And leave our mundane town
To Oakwell or Hillsborough or Millmoor
Or any other football ground.

The bus would be full of men and boys
Of crates of beer and grub,
With rattles and scarves of red and white
The colours of Barnsley Club.

Whatever ground we graced that day
It was always a great occasion,
We stood with the supporters of the other club
There was no segregation.

And yet there were never any trouble
Some supporters had bells or a rattle
And the ground would be full, it were deafening,
They'd be arguing, no fighting, just prattle.

It was normal even at 'Derbys'
To see rattles and hats and scarves
Of both colours, together, all over t'ground
Not like today in two halves.

Whatever the score at the match that day
Of one thing you could always be sure,
There'd be singing and laughing on the bus back to Wath
Next week we'd be back for some more.

Now dad's favourite pastime was t'Buffaloes
At Oak Tree Inn R.A.O.B.
Where he'd go every Saturday evening
Upstairs in a room at t'Oak Tree.

He had all sorts of fancy regalia
He took with him on Saturday night,
There were medals and ribbons and sashes,
He must have looked a wonderful sight.

The Buffs meant a lot to my father
They looked after him when he was ill,
They sent him to go convalescing,
I remembering him going, now, still.

They sent him on holiday to t'seaside
To Weston-Super-Mare
To a Rest Home owned by the Buffaloes,
He said how he'd liked it there.

It were lovely that Dad had this holiday
But I tell you it's really quite sad,
That the holiday he went to in Weston
Was the only one he ever had.

Now mam and dad never had holidays,
It's something they weren't interested in,
So we never had a holiday together
And that includes Betty and Ken.

We always had a Buffs Party
At Christmas, upstairs at the pub,
We had sandwiches, jelly and trifles
And buns and all sorts of grub.

As soon as the eating was over
The lights in the room would go out
There was laughing and screaming and shouting
We didn't know what the fuss was about.

The lights came on again shortly,
For a moment it dazzled our eyes,
And there stood old Father Christmas,
The pub landlord in clever disguise.

We cheered and we laughed and we all gathered round
To see what he'd got in his sack,
We all got a present all neatly wrapped
Then he left with his sack on his back.

We'd go home that night feeling happy and good
Still full up with cream buns and jelly
And when we got home we would go straight to bed
And mam would say, 'God Bless thi belly.'

I remember one day, a time so far away,
My dad and I had a chat.
'I don't care what tha does when tha leaves school
But tha not gooin dahn pit and that's that.'

I can remember dad saying it with such passion
As he clenched his fist in the air
And he smashed it down on the table
Ee! I nearly fell off mi chair.

Everything bounced on the table
Cup left saucer, knife left plate
And sugar leapt out of its basin
And dad's gesture had sealed my fate.

'I don't want to go down pit, dad,' I said,
'I want to sit down and do drawings
Of houses and factories and churches and pubs
And office blocks, hotels and things.'

So it's down to mi dad that I didn't go down t'pit
And I went on to do something different,
Whilst all of mi pals said I was daft
But to me that was totally indifferent.

A FLAT-CAP, SNAP-TIN AND DUDLEY

When I were a lad, I remember mi Dad
Going to work at the mine,
On days, on nights or on 'afters'
4 a.m., 2 p.m. or at nine.

They were always the same, his clothes and things,
They never varied one day,
I never saw him in ought different
It's rubbed off on me in a way.

I remember the old brown 'mack' that he had
All black where the buttons were sewn
Where he used his coal-covered fingers
To fasten the buttons each dawn.

It was black all round the buttons
And the collar was mucky anawl,
It was like that as long as I remember
Life at the pit were no ball.

He wore a flat-cap like a 'pancake'
That covered his head every day
But black streaks ran down his face when it rained,
'Bloody weather,' he'd often say.

His shoes were always shiny though,
Immaculate in every respect,
And when he came home they were always the same
His feet were always well bedecked.

'Look after thi shoes lad,' he'd always say,
'If tha cleans 'em they'll always look neat,
So mek sure tha cleans 'em every day
Then thi shoes'll look nice on thi feet.'

It were amazing how dad looked after his shoes
In fact he would 'mend' them himself
He bought his own leather and his own 'Hobbin Foot'
And a sharp knife that he kept on a shelf.

I remember the smell of leather
And the squeak of leather on knife
And leather offcuts all over t'place
As dad brought shoe soles back to life.

I remember though in my earlier childhood,
Dad wore wooden clogs on his feet
Wi metal bases shaped like horseshoes
I could hear him walking, at t'top e street.

And when him and his mates came home from work
A thunderous noise would ensue,
With sound of clog irons on pavements
There could have been a dozen or two.

Now, you couldn't go to t'pit without taking some snap
To eat in your ten minute break,
Hundreds of feet down under the ground
So a 'snap-tin' you had to take.

Now 'snap-tin' is Yorkshire for Food-Box
It was the only one Dad ever had,
It was made from tin all worn-out and old
And shaped like a slice of bread.

He carried his snap-tin on a hook on his belt
That slapped on his bum when he walked
It contained his bread and dripping
Or bread, not with butter, but Stork.

He also had a 'Dudley'
To carry his water in
This was shaped like a flask's inside
And this was worn-out like his snap-tin.

I often think of my father
Eating his food in the mine,
Covered in coal, pink lips and pink eyes
And the dust in the 'light' thick and fine.

You look at the Health Regulations
That we have to contend with today
And think of the way that Dad ate his snap
Down in the shaft every day.

With his hands all covered in coal dust and grime
And grease and snot and sweat,
He'd to eat his snap without washing his hands
And without giving it a thought I bet.

Then home he would come with his snap-tin and Dudley
And there in the house they would stay
Until it was time to fill them again
To take down the mine the next day.

So when you are eating your breakfast
Or your dinner or your tea as well
Just think of the hard-working miner
Eating his snap in 'Hell.'

PHILOSOPHY

When I look back in time and think of mi dad
And the things that he never had,
I realise that we could have lived better,
Ee! it makes mi feel quite sad.

As I said, he smoked like a chimney
And he liked a drink as well
I suppose if he hadn't we'd have money to spend,
But remember that he worked in Hell.

I can't begrudge him his Guinness
Or his Woodbines either that's true,
Or his visits to t'pub every evening
With his pals, 'cos they did t'same too.

I try to remember the people I knew
And when I stop to think
I can only remember one person
Who didn't smoke and drink.

That person was my dear old mum
And I have to stop and pause,
Because she died at sixty,
Lung cancer was the cause.

Yet dad, he lived to eighty-six
And he caused all the smoke,
It makes you realise dunt it,
That passive smoking is no joke.

But mi dad only spent the money he'd got
On rent and food and power
And what was left he spent on him
At the pub where he spent many an hour.

Mi dad and his pals knew all about work,
Hard graft, down in hell, it weren't funny,
But they knew what to do when they'd finished their shift
They lived life to the full and spent money.

Dad knew what to do when he'd finished down t'pit
After several long hours of horror
'Sithee, it's no good saving for a rainy day
'Cos tha might be dead tomorrow.'

So he spent what he earned, it weren't that much,
But just what he earned and no more
So we didn't have paddles at t'seaside
And we only had lino on t'floor.

That's why mi dad had no luxuries,
No T.V., no car, no phone
He just had his Guinness and Woodbines
And his Buffs where he went on his own.

He would never have owt on t'weekly,
No H.P. or Providence cheque,
'If tha can't afford it, don't 'ave it'
Or else tha'll be a nervous wreck.'

I know why dad never had owt
It was because of his philosophy
That he stuck to for all of his lifetime
In some ways, it's rubbed off on me.

I can always remember dad saying,
'Come 'ere lad, 'ave summat to say
So pin back thi lugoles an' listen,
It'll stand thi in good stead one day.'

'If tha ent got the money, dunt 'ave it
Tha'll be better off gooin without,
IT DUNT MATTER IF THA ENT GOT NOWT
AS LONG AS THA DUNT OWE NOBODY OWT.'

It's a good job mi mam were different
Though she never told mi dad
That she'd taken on hire purchase
For the first telly we ever had.

Mi mam worked doing school dinners
So she earned some extra 'bread'
She went out and rented a telly.
If mi dad knew she'd be dead.

I suppose that mi dad's philosophy
That he stuck to all his life
Meant, we didn't have any luxuries
But we didn't have financial strife.

CHAPTER THREE

MY MAM

My mam was a funny woman
Funny, not 'ha ha' but shish,
You didn't really know how to take her
And her life with my dad was a mish.

She was small like my dad but plumper,
No make-up or jewellery worn,
She was never a follower of fashion
And looked at 'fast' women with scorn.

She never wore owt but a pinny,
Flat shoes and ankle socks too,
With a fashionless dress and cardy
That she'd had for a year or two.

Her life with my dad was a shambles,
They would argue and bicker and fight
Until dad raised his voice full crescendo
Then mam would start crying alright.

I used to think dad was an ogre
But it's only of late that I know
That mam would nag dad to distraction
And that's when the verbals would flow.

For all this my mam was a softie,
Her heart was so generous and good
She'd give anyone her last penny
Especially to me her own brood.

Her hobbies were beetle and whist drives,
Knitting and pictures and such,
But cooking and sewing and playing at house
She didn't really care very much.

I know she was proud of her children,
On occasions embarrassingly so,
She would stop a neighbour while walking
And say 'Here's my son does tha know?'

Yet we spent many hours together
Mi mam and me all on our own
Going to t'pictures and beetle and whist drives
And going shopping to town.

The best place we went to was 'Donny',
On Saturdays we'd go on the bus
We went to 'Dolls' Hospital' in t' High Street
Where mi mam would make quite a fuss.

She'd always buy me a 'Dinky'
In the form of a bus or a car
To add to my extensive collection,
My mam was really a star.

Yet for all this love and this kindness
I could never understand why
Mam never liked parties or visitors
That's where the main problems lie.

I loved to bring friends home for supper
For parties and snogging and such
But mam said she didn't really like it
So I never did it that much.

I felt that she didn't want to lose me
Because I was all that she'd got,
I suppose that the pictures and shopping and whist
Were her whole life but then, maybe not.

The pictures were her main amusement
She'd take me at least once a week
To Mexbrough or Wombwell or Swinton
Or Wath or West Melton we'd sneak.

It's because of these visits to t'pictures
That I'm such an expert today
On names of old film stars and actors
And films that were shown yesterday.

We even went to the pictures sometimes
In afternoons or on shopping day
Then we'd come out of t'pictures at teatime
Eyes dazzled wi t'sun blazing away.

THE BUS

I can still remember the bus queues
We'd stand in to wait for our bus
To take us back home after shopping
When home, Dad never made any fuss.

I can remember the inside of buses,
They always seemed to be full,
Cos' people didn't have cars in those days
And the cars they had were quite dull.

I can still remember t'conductor
With his bag and his little machine,
It was silver and strapped to his middle
Dispensing the tickets so clean.

Mi mam used to make mi get up off mi seat
If a woman was stood in the aisle
I'd sit on mam's knee or stand up mi sen
Then she'd take mi seat and smile.

I remember the smell of fumes in mi nose
And the noise of the engine so much
And the little round heater with its grille at the front,
That was extremely hot to the touch.

I was really quite interested in buses
And when I was out with mum
I would run on in front making noises
Like 'peep-peep' and 'brum-brum-brum.'

I would stop very often at lamp posts
Just like a bus at a stop
Then as soon as mam caught mi up again
I'd change gear and off I would hop.

The only thing wrong with being a bus,
Especially when you're out at nights,
Is how can you expect to be seen
If you haven't got any lights?

'A torch is the answer,' I said to mi mam.
She said, 'I don't have the money'
So I had just to carry on as before,
A bus without lights is not funny.

One day whilst out shopping I was waiting for mam
I was sat on a wall in the town,
I saw something move at the back of the wall
It was paper so I quickly jumped down.

I went to the bush where the paper was stuck
And mi words just stuck in mi throat
I couldn't believe it when I picked it up,
'Flippin eck it's a ten shilling note!'

I knew it couldn't be anybody's
For there wasn't anybody about
So I ran across to the 'torch' shop,
I had a torch in mi hand when I came out.

I was gob-smacked! I couldn't believe it,
At last I'd got a flashlamp,
It only cost mi two shillings
I'll save the rest for Scout Camp.

When mi mam came I told her about it,
'You little devil,' she said,
'Tha shouldn't go and spend all that money
Tha can gi mi rest instead.'

So I gave mi mam t'other eight shillings
But I just didn't care a damn
Cos I'd bought missen some new headlights
For mi bus, so I changed gear and ran.

I remember one day that some lads got to know
I played buses and looked a right Dick,
So they must have decided to have a good laugh,
They decided that they'd play a trick.

Then one afternoon they knocked on our door
'Is your Malc in? We just want to see him'
'No,' said mi Dad, 'What does tha want?'
'Will he sell us a bucket of steam?'

You'll have noticed by now that I spent quite some time
Wi mi mam and a bit wi mi dad
But to think that we spent none together as three
Is really terribly sad.

I'll never forget all mi buses
Whether walking or running or riding
Or whether I played 'em in bed or in t'street
They're still in mi mind abiding.

Footnote.
When I look back in time and think about my playing buses in the street
or on my bike or on my bed (see Private Games) I realise that I wasn't
playing at buses, I *was* a Bus.

29

A FETTLING AND WASHING DAY

When I were a lad Mams worked hard
Washin and fettlin and stuff,
And sometimes I would help her
There'd be times when she'd had enough.

I remember the fireplace in the 'room',
A Yorkshire range black and stout,
It had an oven door with 'silver' hinges
And a fire that never went out.

There'd be a kettle constantly boiling
And a hearth with a coal scuttle in
Stood on a old newspaper
And a shovel, old, rusty and thin.

There was a mantlepiece up at high level
Too high for me to reach.
'Don't thee try reachin up there or owt
Or tha'll tipple in t'fire,' she'd preach.

The mantlepiece had a cloth on,
A mucky old thing in red,
I don't think it was ever taken down to wash
It was left there for years instead.

The hearth had a lovely brass fender
It would encompass the hearth right snug,
It was there to prevent falling embers
Burning mam's homemade peg rug.

'Does tha want to black lead t'stove lad?'
Mi mam would shout in a fluster,
'Then tha can brasso yon fender
So get thissen a duster.'

Ee I made that stove look just like new
I 'blacked' it with skill and pace,
And the fender was so bright and shiny
Like in a mirror I could see mi face.

'That's lovely,' said mi mother,
'Tha's done a good job theer
If tha wants to 'elp wi t'washin
Get thissen in 'ere.'

Now in those days when doing the washing
You didn't have soap powder and washer,
You had a tub, a boiler and mangle
And a rubbing-board and 'posher.'

We didn't have hot water from a tap
We put water in the copper to boil
We had a big coal fire beneath it
To help mi mother's toil.

She'd use a great big bucket
To transfer the water to the tub
Then the clothes with a block of Fairy Soap
On the rubbing-board she would rub.

She'd let me use the 'posher',
The rubbing-board as well,
The water in the tub was grey
And had a funny smell.

She'd wash some clothes in t'boiler,
Mi dad's he wore down t'pit
She couldn't wash 'em in t'tub though
Cos they were full of coal dust and grit.

She'd put them thro' the mangle
And squeeze out the surplus wet
Then hang them on the rack to dry
But we weren't finished yet.

We had to empty all the water,
All grey and smelling horrid,
By bucket down the stone pot sink
Our wash day was quite torrid.

I think of all those racks of clothes
Hanging there to dry,
Dripping and steaming in t'kitchen
It makes me want to cry.

Ee! I remember these wash days so clearly
And the things that I did for my mother
There were so much steam in our kitchen
That you couldn't see one end from t'other.

But now those days are ended
I wish mam was here to see
And enjoy the many luxuries
That there didn't used to be.

THE SHOPPING CHORE

When I were a lad a long time ago
I remember it so clearly
I'd help mi mam wi shopping and like
I don't think I liked it really.

When I were a lad in the forties
You could go all o'er t'place by yer sen,
You didn't need to worry about strangers
There weren't many a them about then.

So goin' to t'shop for yer mother
Was a natural thing that were done
Even though it was an intrusion
Into your playing out and fun.

I could always hear mother shouting,
As she stood there looking about,
'Eh lad come 'ere, ah want thi,
'Urry up or tha'll get a clout.'

'Ah want thi to go t'shop for mi.'
'Aw mam gi or, am playing.'
'Sithee if tha dunt come 'ere sharpish
Tha gonna finish up prayin.'

'I weant be long,' I'd say to mi pals
And they'd all be shouting and grumbling
But they were no better when their mother called
And they'd be all moaning and mumbling.

'Now 'eres thi note of what I want
And t'money's wrapped up inside.
Make sure tha comes back wi mi change
Or else ah'll tan thi 'ide.'

So off I'd run with mi note and money
Round to the corner shop,
Sometimes I'd run all t'way there and back
But if I met a pal I'd stop.

I remember quite well when I got to the shop
On the door a brass handle and sneck,
You'd push like hell to open it
You nearly broke yer neck.

The bell would ring and I'd fall into t'shop
I'd be sprawled out there on t'floor,
'Yer clumsy bugger,' the man would say
'Get thissen up and shut door.'

So up I would get with note in hand
And go to the counter right quick
I'd hold up mi hand wi t'note clinched in fist
And the man would take it real slick.

Now I couldn't see over t'counter,
It was up there above mi head,
So I stood there wi one foot kicking t'counter
Picking mi nose and scratching mi head.

There were all sorts of things mam wanted
And he put 'em all in a bag
And he handed it over t'counter with ease
When I took it mi arm would sag.

There'd be black lead for t'stove, brasso for t'fender,
Dolly blue and cigs for mi Dad,
And big blocks of green soap marked 'Fairy'
And for t'steps a scouring pad.

''Ere tha are,' the man would say,
'Thi change's inside t'bag
So off tha goes, get off 'ome,
Don't go and dawdle and lag.'

So off I'd go carrying mi load
Swapping it from hand to hand,
Putting it down or dragging it,
It was heavy you'll understand.

''Urry up,' mi pals would say
When I had reached our road,
'Tha'r 'olding t'game up, 'urry up,
Gi thi mam thi load.'

''Ere yer are mam, there's yer change
Can ah go back aht to play?'
'I tha can, thank yer lad
Tha's done thi chores for today.'

CHAPTER FOUR

MY BROTHER AND SISTER

Now I had a brother called Kenneth
And a sister called Betty as well,
Whilst Kenneth was always my hero
Our Betty made my life Hell.

Now Ken, I was ten years his younger,
And Betty just eight years that's all,
Sometimes I would be very happy
But sometimes unhappy an awl.

Kenneth was always my guardian
And took me wherever he went
In pram or in pushchair or even on foot
Many hours together we spent.

The day came when Ken was to leave me
To Air Force he was destined to go,
He left me in charge of our Betty
It was a sad and terrible blow.

I was seven years old when he left me
And I still remember today
The terrible sadness and torment
That my Kenny was going away.

I couldn't let him go and I wouldn't
So I clung to his legs hard and fast
But he just had to go, so he left me,
And my joy was a thing of the past.

He went to the Air Force near Bedford
To fly Lancasters and Jets
It was the best thing he did I am certain
And I know he had no regrets.

But to me, a snotty nosed urchin,
Who was losing a part of his life,
I couldn't stop crying for ages
And I didn't know how I'd survive.

I remember so clearly the heartache I had,
It seems just like yesterday,
That I'd no longer have my Kenny
And that my hero had gone away.

And now I faced a new terror
How I'd survive I couldn't tell
Cos I'd got a new 'governess', mi sister,
Who was going to make my life Hell.

BETTY

Our Betty was always a misery
And I was put into her care
She bossed me about from morning till night
She really got under my hair.

'Tha not gooin to school with thi face black,'
Our Betty said right from the start,
'So thad better get used to the fettlin'
I'm gonna mek thi face smart.'

She sat me on t'sink in a tizzy,
A stone one, all cold and unkept,
She rubbed mi face hard with a dish cloth
Until I just broke down and wept.

'What's up wi thi nar,' said our Betty,
'Thi roorin al not mek mi stop
I'm gooin to clean aht thi earoles
An then al tackle thi neck.'

She then took hold of my ear lobe
In one hand, a pin in the other,
She cleaned out my ears with t'pin and –
Oh I wish I'd still got mi brother!

I'm surprised that my ears are still hearing
As well as they still are today
After all the scraping and gouging
That our Betty did yesterday.

I suppose that she thought she was doing
The best things for me that she could
By having clean earholes, neck, hands and hair
I would turn up at school looking good.

I put up wi mi sister, I had to,
She certainly made my eyes blink
But one day my nightmare ended
I got too big for sittin' in t'sink.

But when I got a little bit older
Things got a little bit better one day
Cos mi sister were gooin to get married
And she was going to live away.

She let me be a groomsman
On the day that she got wed,
Riding in a car at t'front
'By eck that's great,' I said.

Ee I couldn't get to sleep for days
I can still remember it nar
Because it's the first time ever
That I had been in a car.

The day came for the wedding
I jumped up and down with joy,
Mi sister would be leavin home
For good, oh boy! oh boy!

We took them to the station
And as we said goodbye
As soon as Bet got on the train
I'm afraid I started to cry.

I cried and cried, I couldn't stop,
My mind was in a hell of a muddle,
Then Betty jumped down from the train
And came and gave me a cuddle.

'Don't worry,' said our Betty,
'We won't be long away
And when we're settled in Pontefract
You can come to us and stay.'

It goes to show, that even though
Our childhood may be filled with horror,
That family ties abide inside
And will still be there tomorrow.

CHAPTER FIVE

RELATIVES

I had lots of uncles and aunties
And cousins all over the land
At Wath and Wombwell and Mirfield
And some were really quite grand.

I got on right well with mi cousins
And mi uncles and aunties an awl,
And whenever we spent time together
We always had a ball.

The uncles on mam's side were Gilbert
And Bill and Tom and Fred,
I was told I was t'image of t'latter
'Tha's image a Fred,' mi mam said.

I only knew two of dad's brothers,
My uncles Reuben and Bill,
And then there were his sister Sally
And Charlie her husband as well.

Now mi mam's brother Bill lived at Wombwell,
His wife were mi auntie Min,
They had seven children, mi cousins
There were always a terrible din.

I loved to go and stay wi 'em
We had such a wonderful time,
Mi auntie was noisy and common
But her love and affection were prime.

Now Min was a really big woman
And she shouted and bawled at us all
She'd hit us and clout us on lug 'oles
But we always had such a ball.

The tablecloth was yesterday's newspaper
And the milk never had any jug
It was left on the table in t'bottle
And my uncle had a pint tin mug.

I wasn't quite used to kerfuffles
Or laughing or swearing or din
But I liked it, loved it, especially
When I was called 'little bugger' by Min.

Now my uncle Bill was a belter
He was blonde and really quite tall,
He looked a lot like mi brother
But he wasn't like him at all.

Now uncle Bill was a miner,
I'm afraid he was really quite ill,
That's why they were poor, he wasn't working,
He was happy and jolly though still.

He did the most wonderful paintings
They were hung on the wall all around
It's a travesty that a man with such talent
Had never an Art Scholarship found.

Sometimes he would call me 'Eh Malcolm,
Come ere and help me in part
Ah want thi to pull hard on mi finger.'
So I did and he'd make a loud fart.

Now they say that there isn't any justice
And with that I must totally agree,
Cos my uncle died young of cancer,
I doubt if he'd reached forty-three.

All of my uncles died early
At least those that worked in the pit,
Of cancer and strokes and thrombosis
And 'lung dust', they were never that fit.

There were only one man who survived them,
The eldest and smallest of all,
Mi dad with his sixty-a-day Woodbines
And his chest and his lungs full of coal.

Mam's last brother, Fred, lived in Sowerby,
Sowerby Bridge near Halifax town
They lived in a terrace on a very steep hill
That was cobbled all way up and down.

Again uncle Fred were a comic
And so was Gladys his wife,
I think they were probably poorest in t' lot
They too had a hell of a life.

Uncle Fred he smoked like a chimney
He was tall and thin as a lath.
Mi mam said 'Ee tha are like 'im.'
And I was but I was more fat.

I didn't go to stop there much either
I guess it was too far to go
They only had gas for their lighting
And they didn't have hot water, oh no.

They had six kids who all slept together
In one bedroom, in't two up two down,
With all coats on their bed used as blankets
And another for their eiderdown.

I did stay there once, I was happy,
I fact I had a ball
Cos when I went to bed after supper
I slept in their bed an awl.

Now mi dad's youngest brother called Bill,
I think he got on with him best,
He lived with Flo, that's my auntie you know
When I spent time with them they did jest.

Uncle Bill were ever so funny
And Flo were vulgar but fun,
I spent a lot of time playing there
From morning till day were near done.

Now Bill he too liked his Woodbines
And his beer and he worked at t'pit
But he didn't live too long either
But while he did he made sure he enjoyed it.

When I sit down and think of my family
I can't help myself but to say,
That although they really had nothing
They got on with their lives every day.

I suppose you might say we were common
And noisy and vulgar and coarse
But we really didn't hurt anybody
Wealth and arrogance was worse.

They lived together as family
And whilst they didn't always get on
They were always there for each other
To prevent them from being stepped upon.

It really fills me with sadness
To think that my uncles died young
Because of their toils and their labours
Denied their grand-daughters and sons.

I suppose that the time I spent with them
Through the years, has helped me to see
That the love and the fun and laughter
Were very precious to me.

CHAPTER SIX

SCHOOL DAYS - THE INFANTS

When I started school in the winter
I was stepping into the unknown,
There were no pre-school playgroups in those days
And you went to school on your own.

You weren't taken to school by your parents,
You set off and went on your own,
But you always met up with your school friends
So you were never really alone.

Nobody had cars in those days
Certainly not in our neighbourhood
So there was no chance of being dropped off
By mam or by dad in a Ford.

You just set off to school, even in winter,
In rain or in snow or in sleet
And many's the time you'd be sat in the class
All day with wet hair, clothes and feet.

We had to cross a main road every day
To get to our school in Park Road,
There were no 'lollipop' ladies to see us across
In those days, to and from our abode.

To be fair though there wasn't the traffic
That there is on our roads today,
Only the well-off had cars in those days
The 'miners' didn't get enough pay.

There were never such things as abduction
Or sexual assault or rape
Because there were no sexy films at the flicks
Or on telly or video tape.

We didn't even have televisions,
The pictures were all that we had,
The worst that you had were crime thrillers
That you saw with your mam or your dad.

I always stayed for school dinners
Right from the very first day,
We sat at a really long table
After dinner we'd go out to play.

I can't really say how the food was
But with the shortage of food that we had
It must have seemed like a banquet
To every school girl and lad.

You didn't have a knife and a fork then
But a spoon and pusher to push,
You'd push the grub onto the spoon like
Then spoon the food into your mush.

We always had milk in a morning,
It was kept in a crate by the door,
You had it in right little bottles
Which you drank through the top with a straw.

I can remember so clearly the smell of the milk
And the noises the children would make,
The sipping and gurgling as they got to the end
As they emptied the bottle right quick.

I can remember one more thing we had every day,
And I cringe when I think of it now,
Was the daily dose of Cod Liver Oil
That the teacher forced on us, the cow.

You stood in a row with your eyes popping out
Thinking 'I'm gonna be at t'front soon,'
And when you get there she'd say, 'Open up'
And she'd ram it in your gob wi a spoon.

When you think of the health regulations
That we have to contend with today,
In our day we all took a dose from t'same spoon
Today, God, there'd be right hell to play.

Now, every afternoon in the infants
We all had to lay down to sleep
For an hour or so on campbeds
Set out in rows two deep.

I can remember the smell of the blanket
And the material rough on mi face
You couldn't do any laughing or talking
If you did you got put in your place.

That's all I remember of Infants,
Except the first day I was there,
And that's instilled in my memory
So vivid and detailed and clear.

CHAPTER SEVEN

MY FIRST DAY AT SCHOOL

My first day at school was in t'Infants
At Wath Park Road Junior School,
It was certainly very eventful,
You talk about looking a fool.

I was fine when I walked in the classroom
Miss Marshall was our teacher that day
Her hair was tied in a pigtail
More than that I really can't say.

I'd only been there thirty-minutes
And all was going quite well
When suddenly from my Nether Regions
There came the most terrible smell.

'Whose that?' said Miss Marshall in earnest,
'Come along, somebody tell me then.'
I put my hand up and said, 'Please miss
I think that 'av ba-ba'd me sen'.

'Ba-ba'd thissen?' said Miss Marshall,
Increasing her ravings and rants,
She put her hand down me trousers
And found out I'd crapped in my pants.

'Oh dear, dear, dear', said Miss Marshall,
She really talked awfully posh,
'We had better go to the cloakroom
And there I can give you a wash.'

I'm afraid by this time I was crying
I was in a hell of a mess
With crap down mi legs passed my kneecap
And inside mi sock I would guess.

She stood by mi desk in a tizzy
The smell must have been pretty bad,
Her nose was sort of twitching
And her eyes looked sickly and sad.

With the hand that was still not affected
By the gunge that she'd found down below
She led me out of the classroom
As fast as I could go.

Now to try to walk fast isn't easy
Especially if you're little like me
With your legs wide apart like a Jockey
And crap running down past your knee.

At last we had made it to safety,
After passing thro' sniggers and laughs,
To the cloakroom with coat hooks and benches
Wash basins, toilets and draughts.

'Please stand on that bench,' said Miss Marshall
I think she was feeling quite vexed,
She undid mi 'snake' belt round mi middle
And proceeded to take down mi kexs.

I know that she washed round my 'Privates'
To wash all my troubles away
But what happened to trousers and pants and the like
I still do not know to this day.

CHAPTER EIGHT

THE JUNIORS AND SENIORS

Now I've already forgotten to tell you
That when I was a baby aged two
I had to start wearing glasses
Cos' of measles that I caught good and true.

The measles affected mi eyesight
So much so that mi left eye went crossed,
So the glasses they gave me were different
One lens were clear, one embossed.

In actual fact it was plastic
In pink to replace the lens
So it meant that one eye was obscured
The embarrassment was very intense.

And also to make matters worse,
Though with good intent I suppose,
My mum wrapped some wool round the bridge of the specs
To prevent any soreness to my nose.

Now I don't need to tell you I'm sure
What a 'spectacle' I must have looked
For confronting 'the Big Boys' in the Juniors
My goose was undoubtedly cooked.

I was now at the tender age of seven
And was still exceptionally small
So when entering the Junior playground
I stood no chance at all.

I'd been wearing these glasses a while now
In the Infants and while playing out too
So I never thought anything about it
I didn't know that ther'd be a 'to do'.

The juniors also joined with the seniors
In the playground for their playtime fun
And that made things worse for us 'littlies'
So it meant that we'd be on the run.

We went out to play in the playground
Oblivious of the 'enemy' within,
We didn't know big lads got you,
So soon, there was a terrible din.

The 'big boys' came into the playground
Shouting 'gallows gallows' right loud,
We didn't have a clue what they meant though
But soon we were going to find out.

Now being a 'four eyes' was horrid
They called you 'four eyes' in verse
But when they saw I was a 'three eyes'
That made things even worse.

They tried to get me cornered
Shouting 'Three eyes, three eyes, come 'ere
'We're gooin to put thee on't gallows!'
'Put me on't gallows,' I said, 'No fear'.

Now although I was only little
I was a nippy little kid
So I made sure that they didn't get me
And ran to the classroom and hid.

'We'll get thi later three eyes,' they said,
Then they chased another lad around
'Till they caught him to take him to t'gallows
After they caught him in a corner on't ground.

Now the gallows were really a handrail
Round a platform with steps leading down,
They led from classrooms to playground
All wood and stained a dark brown.

They got hold of the lad that they captured
And took him, one on each arm,
Then they hung him by his hands from t'handrail
So his feet were dangling down.

Two lads held his hands on the handrail
While another two tickled him cruel
Then another would pull down his trousers
Making him look such a fool.

As soon as they took down his trousers
They'd then let him down and run off
Then chase round to find one more victim
Having a laugh and a scoff.

It was my turn at afternoon playtime
A big lad, wi muscles like stone,
He chased me round t'playground and got me
I'd been walking about on my own.

'Tha gooin on't gallows na specky,
Stop blubbing and come wi me.'
I was crying my eyes out by this time
But I said, 'I'm not comin with thee.'

So a right old tussle was started
And t'other lads said, 'Look, a fight!'
And they stood around in a circle
While he held mi shoulders so tight.

Whilst he had his hands on mi shoulders
I was swinging mi fists in a fury
But I was that small I kept missing
To the amusement of the onlooking 'Jury.'

But then he let go of mi shoulders
And I was in there pummelling his gut
Whilst he beat down on mi shoulders
I went in with hand, head and foot.

By this time I'm sure we were both crying
When suddenly, two hands pulled us apart
It was teacher who'd heard the commotion,
'To my classroom,' he said, 'And right smart.'

Now I know there's a word called 'injustice'
And I'm putting this word to the test
For defending myself from this bully
With the cane I got six of the best.

You remember my first day in t'Infants,
I crapped in mi pants pretty bad,
Then I got caned on my first day in't Juniors
Oh dear, I daren't tell mi dad.

If you got into trouble in those days
With the teachers and you got the cane
If you went home and told dad about it
You got 'thumped' all over again.

As time progressed in our school
I became a four eyes, not three,
With the pink bit disappearing from my glasses
I was now better able to see.

I still remained small for my age though
And I now became one of the boys,
We had a really great time together
Though we didn't have a right lot of toys.

In those days we did things together
Every minute we had was spent out
We didn't do such things as graffiti
For fear of getting a clout.

It's not that we weren't little devils
In fact we could be right little buggers,
But there weren't such things as spray cans,
Mindless vandalism or muggers.

Nobody had owt worth pinching,
No T.V.s or videos and like
And non et cars had radios or ought
And you didn't have to chain up your bike.

We used to just draw on the pavement
Or on walls with chalk that we had,
That teacher might have thrown at us
Or at Christmas from mam or from dad.

We'd write silly things on the pavement
Like 'Malcolm's kissed Molly again'
And as soon as we had a downpour
It would be washed away with the rain.

We never used any bad language
We didn't even know what it meant
And if you ever said words like 'bugger' or 'shit'
You were certainly made to repent.

There was much more discipline in the classroom
Because corporal punishment was done
Like the cane or being hit with a slipper
Or a 'flat hand' on leg – t'wasn't fun.

Mrs Nichols was one for 'flat handing',
We liked going into her classes,
We all tried to sit at the front of the room
So we could watch when she slapped the lasses.

She'd call a bad girl to the front
And lean her over the table
She'd lift up her skirt and her blue knicker leg
As high up the leg as she was able.

She'd return to her desk, 'flat hand' mark on leg,
Whilst we lads made giggles and sniggers
We'd find her at playtime and go over to her
And say to her 'We've seen your knickers'.

It was one way for us to get back at the girls
Who were always so pompous and churlish,
They were bossy, stand-offish and didn't like boys
They were really so childish and 'girlish'.

Most teachers in those days were tough
Not many put up with much cheek
But the odd one would have a hard time
By the kids in the classroom each week.

One teacher who does come to mind
Was the maths teacher, old 'Nobby Clarke',
Who couldn't control one or two
Of the lads who would give him the nark.

John Whitehouse was the main trouble maker
He sat at the back of the class
He would shout things at Nobby to rile him
And he'd made us all laugh *en masse.*

There's a swear word beginning with F
And ending with the letters I.N.G.
If you add to it H.E.L.L.
You'll know what the saying will be.

One day amongst other things
John shouted out loud 'KIN ELL'
He was quiet on the part before KIN
Which is probably just as well.

Now Nobby looked up with a start,
He was quite an amiable feller,
He rubbed his hand over mouth, nose and hair
And said 'Come out the Kinneller'.

This incident was really quite funny,
I can remember it still to this day,
But I never cheeked any teacher
I was too scared in every way.

The most feared of the teachers in school
Was a lady called Miss Darmanin,
She had a bun in her hair and wore glasses
And had a sharp pointed nose and chin.

To us she was 'Ma' Darmanin
And I tell you she filled me with dread,
She was a tough cane-wielding teacher
And if you cheeked her, you were 'dead'.

But John once again was in trouble
For making a noise once again
'Come out Whitehouse' she shouted
Wielding and swishing her cane.

So John came out to the front of the class
'Hold your hand out,' said Ma quite raging,
'I wayn't 'old mi 'and aht for thee,' said John,
'So tha can 'it mi wi' that bloody thing.'

So Ma grabbed his hand to cane him
But John pulled away even more
And before you knew what was happening
They fell in a heap on the floor.

Now Ma was right in a tizzy,
She'd be very upset I would think,
Because we could all see her knickers
With elastic at knees; they were pink.

So John was grabbed by the ear 'ole
And dragged from the classroom real quick
He was taken to the headmaster's study
And there he was given the stick.

Now these incidents were really quite funny
But one of a more serious kind
Happened with John and my mother
And this is still on my mind.

My mam used to work on school dinners,
She'd serve us kids every day,
One day she gave me more pudding
There were often second helpings that way.

Now John saw her give me this pudding
After that there was no pudding left
And John, because he didn't get some,
Was really extremely bereft.

'Ayop Darby come 'ere I want thee,'
Said John in the playground, quite glum
'Thy mam's a right proper bastard
Wi that pudding, not geein' me some.'

I've mentioned that swearing in those days
Was looked on as something quite bad
But 'bastard' was the worst word of any
When I got home I told mam and dad.

It was so bad that word, I couldn't say it,
I was only a kid when all's said and done
So she said the swear words to me
Until she said the right one.

Next day mam went to t'headmaster
And in turn he sent for us
So John and I went to his study
Oh dear, there was a hell of a fuss.

I had to tell the headmaster
Just what John had said to me
And John had to admit or deny it
One way or another you see.

So John admitted he'd said it
And said sorry to mam pretty quick
Then we went back to the classroom
After John had been given the stick.

John and I were always good friends
And remained so even after this,
He went on to be a top engineer
Even after the lessons he did miss.

The worst thing that happened to me
Whilst at school, I will never forget,
Was the theft of my most treasured possession
My collection of cigarette packets.

Now I didn't have many possessions
But of one I was really quite proud,
It was my cigarette packet collection
It must have been the best one around.

The reason why it was so good
Was because of Ken's trips abroad
He would bring me some packets from each place he went
To add to my very large hoard.

Now I had a grey photo album
And I stuck the packets inside,
In alphabetical order
From the countries so far and wide.

One day I took it to school
For a reason I don't know why,
It was left in the cloakroom, so someone
Must have taken it when they went by.

Now later when I went to get it
I found the collection had gone
I was absolutely gob smacked
And I cried till the day was done.

No one did anything about it
Although it was obviously theft,
My parents or teachers weren't bothered
But I had no cig. packets left.

It is difficult for me to tell you
How terribly upset I felt
'Cos the packets were given by Kenny
And I felt such a terrible guilt.

We never found out who took them
And I never saw them again,
I had lost my most treasured possession
My cig. pack collection from Ken.

RESPECT

I was brought up by mi mam and mi dad
In a way that today might seem strict,
And I did what mi mam and dad told mi to do
To avoid any rows or conflict.

It's not that I was some kind of angel
Or had a halo on top of mi head,
In fact I were a right little monster at times,
'You little bugger,' dad often said.

But the difference between us and the kids today
I suppose, when you stop and reflect,
Is they all seem to grow up quicker
And they don't have the same respect.

When I was a lad, I was told by mi dad,
'Eh lad, 'ave less e thi cheek
'If I hear thas been cheeky or caused any fuss
Tha'll get knocked into t'middle e next week.'

Mi dad always seemed like a towering giant
And all t'grown ups they did anawl,
In those days they were allowed to clout yer
So you weren't really cheeky at all.

If you got told off by your neighbour
For going in his garden or worse,
And if you gave him a mouthful like kids do today
By eck you'd soon need a nurse.

They'd just clout you yer see, no messing,
'Yer little sod young Darby,' they'd shout,
Then they'd 'scutch' you on t'head with a big flat hand
So you'd keep your trap shut and say nowt.

So we'd treat our elders with respect
Cos, as I said, they seemed big and tough
And I didn't want mi earole thumping,
Mi dad's thunderous voice was enough.

You'd be scared yer see of them and yer dad
Cos they'd clout you and give you some verbals
But you couldn't tell yer dad, 'Dad ees 'it mi'
We could have done with some pills or herbals.

No! I'm afraid we just had to take it,
The grown ups let you know where y' stood
Cos' you did what you shouldn't and got clobbered
Or you had an halo on yer head and were good.

When you think of what happens with some kids today
If your self or your rights you protect
You'll get battered or bruised or probably worse
Because of the lack of respect.

DISCIPLINE

When I was a lad, I was scared of mi Dad
Cos if I were bad I knew what he'd do
He'd shout and rant and point his finger
And mi act of wrong-doing I would always rue.

I'd get a 'thick ear' if I was really bad
And if I'd done summat I shouldn't 'ave done
And particularly if I'd caused any trouble for t'neighbours
Even if it were only in fun.

It was the same at school when I were a lad,
Cos corporal punishment was allowed then
And teachers could thump yer or give yer some stick
So you really had to behave yersen.

Apart from a few undisciplined kids
The teachers generally filled us with fear
Cos then they'd the power to give you some smack
And to drag you to t'front by yer ear.

Now I think that we were right little devils
Because of some of the things that we did
But most of our 'crimes' were minor,
Things usually done in our day by kids.

Yer couldn't cheek a teacher in those days
Or damage any things in yer class
Cos you'd be made to pay by teacher or t'headmaster
With the cane on yer hand, or yer arse.

You could always tell when a lad had been caned
When you were in t'playground having some fun
Cos he'd come into t'playground shaking his hand
And blowing on his fingers cos they were numb.

It was really quite a deterrent, the cane,
So in general you behaved like the rest,
Otherwise in class you'd be called to the front
And you'd be given 'six of the best.'

Some of the teachers would walk round the class
With the cane in their hand all the time,
Swishing it or bending it double
By eck, their class had no crime.

Manys the time you'd be sat at your desk
Having a joke with your mate
When the cane would come crashing down on the desk
'Be quiet!' the teacher'd orate.

It weren't only t'cane you were scared of,
There were other things that would make yer blubber,
Our gym teacher used to tan yer arse wi a slipper
And some teachers hit you with a blackboard rubber.

You couldn't do ought about it though
Cos Corporal punishment were allowed in that day,
You couldn't go home and say 'Mam, teacher's hit mi'
Not like the kids can today.

If I went home wi mi hand all throbbing
Or mi bum all red and sore
And if I told mi Dad I'd had stick and like
He used to give mi some more.

But I think we were better off for it
Not like the kids of today
Who appear to get away with 'murder'
Unpunished and not made to pay.

Whoever banned corporal punishment in our schools today
Is this country's all time fool
Cos if children don't get 'thumped' at home
At least they'd get thumped at school.

CHAPTER NINE

FOOTBALL AND THE SCHOOL TEAM

Now Harry Hough was my hero
And you might say 'Who is he?'
Well Harry was goalie for Barnsley
And their best player for me.

Whenever I went to Barnsley
To watch my favourite team play
I wanted to be a goalie like Harry
And I'd play at being a goalie all day.

I'd be diving around all over the place
Making an imaginary save
Tipping em over and saving by t'post
By gum I was really quite brave.

I'd be a goalie in the playground at playtime,
I was goalie in our classroom team too,
I would dive up and down on the tarmac
With kneecaps and arms black and blue.

I would go to the playing fields at lunchtime
To watch the school team play,
They'd be practising ready for t'new season
That wasn't too far away.

Now the regular school team goalie
Would never turn up to train
So Ted Drake the captain said, 'Darby,
Does tha want to play at goalies again?'

'If tha does then come dahn and practise
We'll give thee plenty to do.
Tha can be Harry Hough as much as tha wants
While we all pepper shots straight at you.'

Now the lads in the school team were big
They were strong and had muscles an awl
Whilst I were only a tich of a thing,
I weren't much bigger than t'ball.

Now the footballs in those days were leather
And were always has heavy as lead,
You thought you'd been hit with a boulder
If ever it hit you on t'head.

So I was practice goalie
And I had to give my all
While all the team peppered shots at mi,
It was like catching a cannon ball.

Now many's the time whilst catching the ball
Whether in the dry or the wet
That Malcolm with ball after making a save
Would both end in the back of the net.

One day 'Smigger' Milnes and the captain
Said that I should be in the team
So they told me Mr Martin t'gym teacher
That Darby was really quite keen.

'By gum inti little?' said teacher
'Does tha think he'll be alreat?
It's important wi 'ave a good goalie
Look at the size of his hands and his feet.'

'He'll be alreat,' said Smigger,
'Tha wants to see him play
He's been jumpin' and divin' all over t'place
He's been gerrin up off t'floor all day.'

'I'll give it some thought,' said teacher,
Then on that fateful day
Team sheet went up on t'notice board
And my name was down to play.

The goalie was to be Malcolm Darby,
All my mates were right shocked,
But the regular goalie was jealous
So I got barracked and mocked.

'Ahs tha gor in team then Darby?
Thar only a little squirt
And everyone says that thas rubbish.'
Some people do say things that hurt.

But I weren't at all really bothered
And as I pulled my shirt on   ·
I was playing for Wath Park Road Juniors,
I was goalie number one.

I can't think what I'd have looked like
When I got dressed in my kit
With a goalkeeper's jersey too big in the arms
And two men inside it could fit.

And mi shorts were down to mi ankles
Tied up round mi waist with some string
And mi boots were all big and heavy
But I tell you I felt like a king.

We went to the pitch for the kick-off,
It was pouring it down with rain,
The pitch itself was a quagmire
I'd never be the same again.

We were playing at home against Bolton
And they turned up in a 'bus
The teacher said that we'd better play well
Or they would annihilate us.

The football pitch was sloping
And the goal at the bottom part
Was one big pool of water
And I had to make saves in that.

So I stood between the goal posts
With the crossbar towering above
And the rain was pouring on me
I got mud all over mi gloves.

We were under pressure all of the match
There were balls flying everywhere,
I was making saves all over the place
Now I'd got mud in my hair.

I was diving here and diving there
I must have sat in every puddle
And whilst we'd scored two they couldn't get one,
We'd got them right in a muddle.

Now all the time we were playing
Our proper goalie were there
He's standing at the back of the goal where I was
Shouting insults and throwing mud in my hair.

He obviously was very jealous
Cos' he was barracking me all the time
Shouting things like, 'That wer lucky Darby,'
And 'Tha's rubbish – they'll score next time.'

They did get one goal before t'finish
But nevertheless we still won
It was two goals to one in our favour,
It was really a job quite well done.

The ball was so big and so heavy
By the time we'd got half way through
That I couldn't even take goal kicks
I was tired and wet through too.

But we'd beat 'em and that's all that mattered,
I felt 'big' like all t'other guys,
I looked just like Al Jolson really,
Black wi mud, pink lips and blue eyes.

Then we went back to the cloakrooms
To get changed to go home and yet
We didn't have any baths or showers
So we had to go home cold and wet.

Now our gym. teacher/coach Mr Martin
Was feeling right pleased and glad,
He went round to praise the players
And to me he said 'Tha's played a blinder lad.'

Of all the things ever said to me
Those words have stuck in my head
I will never ever forget them
They will remain with me until I am dead.

I felt just like 'Dan Dare' and 'Batman',
I couldn't have thanked him enough,
I could even say to myself 'Malc,
Tha played just like Harry Hough.'

At Monday morning assembly
Which was held in the main school hall
The Head conducted the service
Then he talked about the school football.

He told everyone what the score was
And how we'd all played up to scratch
He said that the team was terrific
And that 'Darby was the man of the match.'

After all this euphoria and stardom
My career was to come to an end,
Not through bad form but misfortune,
Something I just couldn't comprehend.

Unfortunately I caught impetigo,
I had it all over my skin,
I was covered in Blue Gentian Violet
The doctor said, 'Pack the game in.'

My name was again on the team sheet
But this time I just couldn't play
So I went to see Mr Martin,
I was crying nearly all day.

By the time I got my legs better
It was too late to get in the side
And the lad who should have been goalie
Took my place and was playing with pride.

I never got back in the side anymore,
They realised, I think, I was small,
And the lad who'd barracked me so much
Was the goalie cos' he was quite tall.

But I enjoyed it whilst I was playing
And I think I can say with some pride
That whilst in goal for Park Road Juniors
I was never on the losing side.

CHAPTER TEN

MY EARLIEST RECOLLECTION

I remember my earliest recollection
Of life, when I was just two,
It's something I always remember
And something that most kids might do.

One night I was laying in mam's bed
A reason for why, I know not,
Perhaps I'd been crying and bawling,
Perhaps I had crapped in my cot.

I can remember staring at the spindles
At the bottom and top of the bed
And an unshaded light bulb above me
Dangling over my head.

I was lying in bed sucking needles
That mam had been using to knit
But instead of sucking the blunt end
I was sucking the sharp ended bit.

Then in the very next moment,
The end down my throat I did ram,
It stuck in the back of my gullet
I suppose I was cuddled by mam.

I can remember the pain that it caused me
Though it's now over fifty years on
I suppose that mam cuddled and loved me,
After all, I was her baby son.

CHAPTER ELEVEN

WARTIME RECOLLECTIONS

I can remember the smell of the gas masks
That they made you wear during the war,
You had to keep practising putting it on
In case Hitler's bombs came through the door.

They were all like black and rubbery
And you put them on over your head,
They stuck out at the front and had goggles
You could never have worn one in bed.

It was terrible when you were breathing
With this thing on over your nose
It went up and down when you breathed in and out,
It was for your own good I suppose.

I can remember our air raid shelter
It was built in our garden, of tin,
It was actually corrugated iron
And it was round with just a single door in.

I remember going into that shelter,
Bombs falling on Sheffield afar,
It smelt sort of damp and fusty
I can still remember it nar.

We had all sorts of funny sandwiches
Because of the shortage of food
But you ate 'em whether you liked 'em or not
Cos' mam said 'They'll all do thi good.'

It was bread and 'maggi' with sugar on top
That crunched when you took a bite,
There were even bread with condensed milk on
And that stuck to your teeth all right.

We even had bread with lard spread on top
Because we'd no meat to make dripping,
It went down right well with a nice cup of tea
You could eat it while you were sipping.

The sandwiches I liked best though,
And something for which I would beg,
Was a slice of bread and margarine
Topped off with Ministry of Food dried egg.

And when mi mam weren't looking,
I'd take the dried egg out
Then I'd put a spoonful in mi mouth,
If dad knew I'd get a clout.

If ever you were lucky to get some tinned fruit
Or some trifle or blancmange or jelly,
You had to have bread with it 'cos there weren't any cake
Or sweet stuff to put in your belly.

For years and years after the war was all done
If ever you had trifle or such
You still had to have it with butter and bread
Not cake. It soon got too much.

When mam served your jelly there'd be a plate by your side
And on it were slices of bread
And you had to eat them together you see
'It'll help fill thi up,' mam said.

I remember anawl, we had ration books
Without em you couldn't buy 'nowt',
And when you'd used all yer points up
You'd to wait till next month to get ought.

Now sweets at that time were all rationed,
You never had chocolate or such,
You got some at Christmas if you were lucky
In your stocking, although not much.

I can remember when rationing was ended,
Around nineteen-fifty I think,
You could go and look in a sweet shop
And the goodies would make your eyes blink.

I don't think that you can imagine
What it must have been like as a lad
To go into a sweet shop with sixpence
And come out with some sweets feeling glad.

I also remember that queues used to form
When rationing was no longer in
Outside all the sweet shops for chocolate and such,
There was always a hell of a din.

At first all the shops would sell out of their goods
You just couldn't buy any 'spice',
But eventually things were soon back to normal
To buy chocolate and sweets, that was nice.

So never forget when your buying your chocs.
Not to take them for granted,
Cos to get some at all when I was a lad
It made you feel quite enchanted.

It was also quite difficult getting fresh fruit
Like bananas and oranges too
But we had a source of apple supply
From a man who was quite good and true.

Mr Henderson lived across the road from us,
He worked at a big house quite close,
As gardener and general dogsbody
A good job in those days I suppose.

He went to work on his bike every day,
A big rusty sit-up-and-beg,
He was really quite old with a drooping moustache
He was tall and he had a bad leg.

When we got home from school we would sit on the wall
Of a garden at the end of our street,
We were waiting for Mr Henderson to come
With a bag full of apples to eat.

At last he would come pedalling right slow
With a bag on his handlebars hanging,
He'd stop by us kids all sat in a row
On the wall with all our legs dangling.

He'd take down the bag and open it up,
T'was a carpet bag in red and in blue,
It was full to the brim with apples all ripe
And the kids looked aghast and said ooh!

He would hand out the apples one at a time
To the kids now forming a queue,
He would always rub them and polish them up
And you never got less than two.

Now this was our routine most nights of the week
Until the apple season was done,
We'd sit on the wall and eat them all up
Then we would play and have fun.

I don't know why Mr Henderson did it,
Perhaps he felt sorry for us,
But I know that all us kids loved him
For being kind and making a fuss.

THE TRAIN CRASH

I remember one day, not far away,
At Manvers in fact, near to t'pit,
There'd been a train crash and we all made a dash
At t'station they were having a fit.

The London Express had crashed down the bank,
Two carriages forming a 'V',
There was chaos with people all running around,
A body lay near to a tree.

Police cars and ambulances sped to the scene
Bells ringing at a very high pitch,
I stood there in awe when I suddenly saw
Two feet sticking up from a ditch.

It was really quite bad and terribly sad
That so many people had died
It had even been said that a man was found dead
In the toilet still sat down inside.

I can still picture now that terrible scene,
The atmosphere, chaos and smell,
The people, the victims, the 'V' down the bank
I don't want to relive that Hell.

CHAPTER TWELVE

ACTIVITIES

When I think of the days of my youth,
Of my time as a snotty nosed kid,
I remember the things that we hadn't and had,
And the things that we didn't and did.

We didn't have T.V. or Video,
We didn't have a car or a 'phone,
We didn't have records or a player,
We just had a wireless at home.

We didn't have board games like kids have today,
Or computers or mechanical toys,
We had Ludo and Snakes & Ladders though,
And we didn't half make some noise.

We didn't have many books either
There were ones though you could find in most houses,
Rupert the Bear, in his little red scarf
And he always were t'same yellow trousers.

That's why our lives were simple like Rupert,
Well you wouldn't expect owt else would you?
The most violent things we played at were cowboys
But you couldn't play at Rupert, could you?

Our main source of fun was the wireless
At night before we went to bed,
There was music and serials and football
We just listened; sometimes we read.

We had comics like Dandy and Beano
That, I think are around still today,
We'd have it delivered on Saturday
Read it then go out to play.

There was Dennis the Menace and Beryl the Peril
And good old Keyhole Kate,
But my favourite man was Desperate Dan
Who ate 'Cow Pie' from a plate.

There are a few things I remember from t'wireless
That we listened to every time,
Like Dick Barton - Special Agent,
That was on every night at tea time.

Now Dick Barton was a serial
It was on fifteen minutes and then
Each night it would end - Dick in trouble,
Next night he'd be saved once again.

It was really very exciting
And you didn't want it to end
But it did, and you went to bed wondering
How Dick would next night make and mend.

Now I was an 'Ovaltinie'
Cos' I had joined their club,
It was on every Sunday at tea time
Before dad went to the pub.

It was lovely being an Ovaltinie,
You had a code and a book,
And each week they read out a message
It was secret, till at your code you did look.

Yer mam didn't know what the code was
And neither did most of your mates
Unless they were Ovaltinies as well
In which case they too could translate.

Now I'll let you into a secret,
I'm going to tell you the code,
So you can always contact them daily
If ever you're stuck on the road.

Z was 1, Y was 2
And X was number 3
Whilst A was number 26
And D was 23.

So now you know the secret
It is written down in verse,
That the letters of the alphabet
Were numbered in reverse.

We awaited our weekly message
When the numbers were read one by one
We could then work out the message
When all the numbers were done.

You had messages like: 'Help mum daily'
And 'Be a good boy every day'
Then when the programme was over
You'd put your 'badge' on and go out to play.

We had an Ovaltinie song
It introduced the show
We had to sing it at the end
I'll sing it to you so you know.

'We are the Ovaltinies, little girls and boys,
Make your requests we wont refuse you
We are here just to amuse you
Will you share our songs and stories!
Will you share our joys?
(I can't remember this line)
No happier children can be seen
Because they all drink 'Ovaltine'
They're happy boys and girls.'

A programme that's still on today
After 40 years I retort
Is on Saturday afternoon Radio 2
And that is Sports Report.

I never missed Sports Report
Unless I was still at the match
And then I would hurry straight home
Or find a radio for the scores to catch.

Now in those days it wasn't called radio
It was called a 'wireless',
They worked from a box like battery
Without it you were in a right mess.

It was called an accumulator
It was like a small car battery
And every so often it had to be charged
And that was left up to me.

Every week I would take the said battery
To a house in Avenue Road
Where I'd leave it and bring back another
And at home I could discharge mi load.

Ee! I can remember that little square battery
Wi two terminals in red and in black,
It was ever so heavy to carry
I'd be knackered by t'time I got back.

The first television I saw
Was when I was fourteen years old
It was for the Queen's Coronation,
In fifty-three I am told.

I watched it with the Williamson family,
They lived next door but one,
It was certainly better than wireless
When they turned the T.V. on.

It was only black and white telly in those days
And they only had fairly small screens
But we sat and watched in amazement,
It was a wonderful sight to be seen.

I remember still watching that telly
Sat on t'floor in Williamsons 'room',
There were a lot more people wi their eyes poppin' out
'Eyop mam, can we 'ave one soon?'

I was sixteen before we had a telly
Mam rented from a shop in town,
It cost about ten bob a fortnight
After putting a couple of quid down.

I remember getting home at tea time
The T.V. was already on
It was William Boyd as Hoppalong Cassidy
Showing on B.B.C.1.

In those days there was only one channel
There was no I.T.V.
That only came much later
But your set was no good then you see.

So you had to get a new telly
Or a conversion on the one that you had,
You needed a new aerial also
When we got it at last, I was glad.

Ee! watching that telly were magic
Even though t'picture were poor,
And that's when t'term 'T.V. dinner' started
Cos I had a tray on mi knee, sat on t'floor.

I used to have to go shopping
To the Co-op in Sandymount Road,
Mi mam would give me a basket
And a purse with money wrapped in a note.

I can still remember that shop now,
The smell and the sawdust floor,
And the overhead track where the money was sent
By the man you paid at the door.

Now the Co-op would pay a 'divi'
Twice a year or more,
I can still remember mam's number
It was three six four four.

I'll tell you we needed that divi
To buy things we couldn't afford
Like some of life's 'little luxuries'
Not 'trinkets' so you didn't get bored.

Aye! when I think of our simple existence
All mi pals anawl, not just us,
I don't think the kids of today would cope
In fact there'd be a hell of fuss.

But for us, apart from those mentioned
We made up our luxuries and fun,
Well! that's what life's about intit?
When all is said and done.

CHAPTER THIRTEEN

THE WINDOW CLEANING GROCERY BOY

Like any lad I needed more money
To spend on goodies and toys,
There weren't any paper rounds going
They'd been taken by other boys.

Now Mr Williamson wanted a helper
He had a window cleaning round,
He offered me a job on Saturdays
Cleaning windows in the town.

I said that I would take it
It's something I would like,
And maybe with my money
I could save up for a bike.

There was just one stipulation
I had to make to him,
That every other Saturday lunchtime
I had to leave to watch mi team.

That's why I wanted a little job
So I could go and watch Barnsley play,
It cost me a shilling to watch 'em
So I could save up from mi pay.

He paid me a shilling an hour
That's equal to five pence today
But I'd work five hours on a Saturday
So I'd earn five shillings a day.

I suppose I enjoyed the job really,
Climbing up ladders all day,
'Now don't forget to clean in't corners,'
Mr Williamson would often say.

He had a brand new, green pick-up truck
It was a Ford with two seats inside
There were ladders and buckets and leathers in't back
And I was having a ride.

I don't think I'd been in a van before
Not for that matter even a car,
But here I was riding in front
Even though we weren't going far.

I think the truck was the reason
That I took the job on for
Cos' I didn't really like window cleaning
But I liked the money more.

As I said I used to earn five shillings,
If I worked longer I could earn even more,
And when I went home when I'd finished
I kept one and gave me mam four.

Now at this time I was mad for a cycle,
The sporting two wheeler kind,
But I knew that I'd never get one
Mi savings were too far behind.

Ah mean! How can yer save for a pushbike
And save to watch Barnsley anawl?
But I've got to go and see Barnsley at Oakwell
Cos! they're my 'Heroes' after all.

Then one day I went to the grocers
To fetch mi mam some food
And as I looked behind t'counter
My eye saw something good.

There was a mucky old bike with a basket on t'front,
The type you make deliveries on,
It was leaning on boxes in the store at the back
So get asking Malcolm my son.

'Is that thy bike?' I said to the man in the shop
'That one leanin up thear.'
'It is,' said the man, 'it's been there a while
'I've got no delivery boy I fear'.

'I'll do thi deliveries,' I said to the man,
'If I can ride on that bike.'
'Tha can do 'em,' he said. 'When can tha start?'
'I'll start Saturday morn if tha likes.'

So I told Mr Williamson I was leaving
And I thanked him for all he had done,
'I've got a job wi a bike nar tha knows,
It's a blacken wi a big basket on'.

I went to t'shop for a couple of times
Before I started my work
And I cleaned up the bike till it looked just like new
Not one single minute did I shirk.

I started mi job on Saturday morning
Delivering orders around,
I'd fill up mi basket with boxes of goods
Ee! It was a wonderful job I had found.

I was pedalling up here, pedalling down there
Dressed in my blue and white pinny,
I was whistling and singing all of the time
Making a right cacophony.

I only worked Saturday mornings though
But that was plenty enough,
Because I could still deliver mi orders
Then go and see Harry Hough.

After a few weeks at delivering goods
Mr Hines the shop owner said,
'I'm gerrin rid of thi push-bike lad
And I'm gerrin a van instead.'

'But tha not goin to lose thi job, lad,
Even though tha won't have thi bike
Cos' I want thi to deliver in't van wi mi
That's summat I know tha will like.'

I was sorry to lose mi push-bike
But to work in a van, by gum!
It'd be great riding round taking orders
So I went home and told mi mum.

We went all over t'place taking orders
And delivering orders to t'door
But it stretched into Saturday afternoon
So I couldn't see Harry Hough anymore.

I soon began to get very upset
On a Saturday missing mi game
So I told Mr Hines 'I can't come anymore
It's mi football tha knows that's to blame.'

So I packed in my work as delivery boy
I'd really had quite enough
I could now go to Barnsley with mi red and white scarf
And again go and watch Harry Hough.

Footnote.
Harry Hough was Barnsley Football Club's Goalie and he was my hero.

CHAPTER FOURTEEN

RELIGION

Now if you go back in time
To sixteen hundred and ten
You'll find that the Darby family
Lived in Ironbridge then.

My ancestors they are quite famous,
Abraham Darby in fact,
The famous Ironbridge builder
It's still there to this day intact.

But then in the late sixteen hundreds
My ancestor went to work in the pit
At Tipton in the Staffordshire coalfields;
After three hundred years, Dad said, 'That's it.'

The Darby family were Quakers,
Called the Society of Friends,
But in seventeen hundred and fifty
Our Quaker membership ends.

That was because of John Wesley,
The Founder of the Methodist sect,
Who preached in the Ironbridge valley
And gained a lot of respect.

He would also have preached in the coalfields
And the miners would have been simple folk
From John Wesley they'd have found some comfort
Cos' mining then, like wi mi dad, was no joke.

So that's when we became 'Chapel'
And joined the Methodists as such,
Mi parents were Methodists when I was born
But they didn't go to chapel much.

They made sure that I went to chapel
Three times on Sunday in all,
To morning and evening services,
They thought I was having a ball.

I also went to Sunday School
On Sunday afternoon
To learn about the Bible
And how to sing hymns in tune.

I didn't like going to Sunday School much,
I'd rather play football instead,
Or even play cricket in summer
Or maybe an hour in bed.

I didn't think much to evening service
But I had to go anyway
We could always play cowboys when we came out of church
Or go on to the racecourse to play.

I always remember one evening
Whilst singing a hymn from my pew,
The preacher interrupted the service
And said 'I've got some news for you'.

'Today on November the fourteenth,' he said,
'Nineteen forty-eight
Princess Elizabeth has given birth to a son
So we should celebrate.'

The son of course was Prince Charles,
The future King to be,
But what was more important
He had the same birthday as me.

I was thrilled to share his birthday
Even though I was now ten
But if the King doesn't ask me to his party
He's no need to ask me again.

We had a youth club at our chapel
It was called the Inters' Guild,
I don't know why they called it that
Cos' to join you didn't have to be skilled.

I used to go there on Tuesday
But I didn't care for it much,
We used to do crafts and play games and things
And do plays and sing songs and such.

We had a Sunday School outing
A day trip once a year
We'd have a 'bus to the seaside
It would fill us full of cheer.

It was a special day for me
Wherever we would go
Because it was the only time
I went away with mam you know.

The most important happening
In our chapel calendar
Was the Sunday School Anniversary
Which happened once a year.

Now the Sunday School Anniversary
Was a very important thing,
It was held in May on a Sunday evening
And you had to get up and sing.

You had to practise for weeks on end,
Wednesday and Friday night,
And you got into trouble if you didn't turn up
Because you had to get things right.

I hated going to practices
Instead of playing out
But if I ever missed one
I'd get a flippin clout.

'Tha'as to go en practise,'
Mam would say each night,
'Cos' if tha dun't learn words and tunes
Tha'll never gerrit right.'

So I had to go and practise
On warm and sunny nights
And I'd pass mi mates playing football,
It would make me feel uptight.

Now going to chapel on Sunday
For a lad is surely enough.
I mean! How can you practise singing
And still be Harry Hough?

With a week to go to t'concert
Things got even worse
We had to practise every night
To make sure we knew every verse.

At last the day arrived
For the 'spectacle' to begin
And if we haven't practised right
There's going to be such a din.

The chapel is packed to bursting,
The conductor is Clifford Swift
It's too late now for errors, Malc,
If I'm 'flat' there'll be a family rift.

At last Clifford raises his baton
The choir bursts into song,
It'll soon be time for my solo
I hope I don't get it wrong.

Now it's time for the solos,
Several kids will sing a verse,
Some will forget the lines or sing flat
Others will clam up, or worse.

It's time for me to sing my verse,
Clifford raises his baton and looks,
The tune comes out like a nightingale
I'm glad I read mi book.

The evening is a great success
Clifford Swift is very happy
It's a good job that we got it right
Or he'd be very snappy.

'It was a lovely night,' Clifford said, all posh,
'You can now go home to bed.'
'Tha's got to be jokin,' I said to Cliff
'I'm gonna be Harry Hough instead.'

CHAPTER FIFTEEN

'THE BOY SCOUTS'

Now when I reached eleven
Mam said, 'Tha should be a scout.
Ah don't know where they all hang out
But there's one or two about.'

So I joined at Wath St James's
A church on Donny Road,
I joined with Baz our neighbour's son
In fact the next abode.

Our scout hut was a small tin shack
Of corrugated iron sheeting,
It used to let the weather in
Whether rain or snow or sleeting.

Our scoutmaster was called Cyril,
We used to call him 'Skip',
His assistant 'Slim' was tall and thin,
I came up to his hip.

We were all split into small 'Patrols'
Six kids made up the team
And I was in the 'Peewits',
A good patrol t'would seem.

Our uniform was khaki,
Our neckerchief green and gold,
We had a scout badge on't breast pocket
We all looked very bold.

Before each meeting started
We had to stand up straight,
We made the scout salute
Then the scout promise we did orate.

'On my honour I promise to do my best
To do my duty to God and the King
To help other people at all times
And to obey the scout law.'

After we'd made the promise
To God and King and so on
We would drop our three fingers held up in salute
And then we'd burst out into song.

'We're the scouts at Wath St James,
We're the lads with smiling faces,
A mile in style that's our paces
Onward we will go.

'Tests, games and camping,
Tie a reef or bowline,
In our scarves of green and gold
We will never be forgotten.

'Hasty words will not be spoken,
Spirits that will ne'er be broken,
Always smiling that's our token,
Forward Wath St James.'

Now this was our own scout song
It was very rousing stuff
It was sung to the tune 'Men of Harlech'
But three verses were enough.

We would learn to tie knots and put up tents,
We would learn to make fire with two sticks,
We'd learn how to sew on a button
And a bit about scout 'Politics'.

If we liked to earn proficiency badges
We could take an exam or a test,
I took six altogether,
Mam sewed them to shirt arm or shirt chest.

I got swimming and first aid and cooking,
Camping and firefighting an awl,
I also got one for woodsman
For recognising tree and bird call.

To get our badge for swimming
One thing you had to do
Was to practise being a lifeguard
And to rescue someone too.

You'd to dive in with your clothes on
Then take em off whilst floating,
But I couldn't get mi damn clothes off
An all mi pals were laughin or gloating.

I kept gooin under t'water,
Three times I went under and then
Scoutmaster dived into t'water
And I had to be rescued mi sen.

It were mi mam's fault I were in trouble:
'Dunt wear slack clothes, wear 'em tight
Cos slack clothes 'ell hold too much water
So wear 'em too small and tha'll be alright.'

I got mi proficiency badge though,
I think that I got it through pity,
'Tha did alreat,' said t'instructor,
'Mindst thi, tha didn't look too pretty.'

To get the one for firefighting
We'd to spend a day with a crew
At Wath-on-Dearne fire station
Where they gave us plenty to do.

We learnt how to put out a fire
With hosepipe or blanket or sand,
We learnt how to carry a person
Using 'fireman's lift' – it were grand.

We learnt how to get from a room filled with smoke
By crawling on't floor round the edge
Never in the middle, cos' joists might have gone,
But at the walls they would form like a ledge.

We had a right smashing time with the firemen
What I learned might keep me in good stead
In case our house ever caught fire
Or dad fell asleep smoking in bed.

The camping badge was the best one to get though,
You'd to camp one night with a mate,
You were given a route map with mileage
And you didn't have to get back late.

I went on my trip with Baz Harrison,
My neighbour and second best friend,
We'd to walk to a place near Conisbro'
We couldn't wait for the day to end.

We set off to walk on a hot summer's day
With rucksacks and pan and kettle
But if we have to walk as far as they say
We shan't be in very good fettle.

By mid-afternoon we were feeling quite tired
And hot and bothered and sorry
So we thumbed a lift for the rest of the way
And rode in the back of a lorry.

Then we walked a while in the countryside
Looking for a field to camp in,
A farmer said, 'Yer can camp just thear.'
It was a lovely spot, 'reet champion'.

We pitched the tent, then had a meal
Of beans and bread and tea
Then we just relaxed by campfire glow
It was right good fun to me.

Next morning it was raining,
The field was very boggy,
The tent was wet and so were we
I was feeling very soggy.

We packed the gear and set off home
We'd try and catch a 'bus
So off to a Conisbro' 'bus stop
There'll be a 'bus coming for us.

Now Baz he wore a berry,
Its colour was navy blue,
And with all the rain we had that day
It began to lose its hue.

The berry blue ran down his face,
He was a sorry sight,
And I didn't look much better
Mine had shrunk and was tight.

I often think what a sight we'd be
Getting on the 'bus,
Wet, bedraggled and Baz's face
What did they think of us?

But we got our camping badges
And that is all that mattered
When I got home, hot meal and bath
'I'm gonna bed mam, I'm shattered.'

Now camping was the greatest thing
We used to go a lot,
We went to various places
But I had a favourite spot.

We used to go to 'Squirrel Wood'
It wasn't too far away,
At other side of Doncaster,
We'd get there in a day.

I will never forget the smell there was
Of nettles and burning wood
And even when I smell them now
My memories start to flood.

We'd either go to annual camp
Or for a shorter stay,
Which ever one we went on
It was great fun anyway.

Each scout troop had a clearing
With its name up on a post
So that when you came to camp
You really couldn't get lost.

We always went by lorry,
We'd be all piled in the back
On top of tents and billy cans
And rucksacks which we had to pack.

I can remember the noise of the lorry,
The engine and changing gear,
The smell of nature and petrol
And the wind on my face and my hair.

We'd sing songs all the time we were travelling,
We were all so happy you see,
And we'd turn into t'entrance of 'Squirrel Wood'
With its smell of nettle and tree.

I can remember the smell of canvas tents
And the clatter of pans and pots
And the thud of rucksacks as they fell on the ground
And the choosing of the best tent plots.

For t'first half hour they'd be arguing
As soon as we'd unloaded all t'gear
'That's my plot Darby, bugger off,
'Tha can't put thi tent up thear'.

But in the end it was decided
The Scoutmaster would have t'best spot,
So we'd have to find another place
Suitable for our own tent plot.

Ee! many's the time I've slept on a slope
And many times rolled out of bed,
Many times I've had a twig up mi arse
Or a tree root under mi 'ead.

Now the Leaders would make out a rota
Of the jobs that we had to do
We had to muck in together and do 'em,
If we didn't there was a right todo.

There was cooking, pot washing and collecting the wood
For the fire for cooking the beans,
There was cleaning the tents, the site and the like
And also digging latrines.

The latrines would be dug in an overgrown place
So you were hidden when you did your stuff,
You had a can with some liquid to pour in the hole
When you'd finished the smell would be rough.

When one latrine was full up
You'd to dig another quick
Then fill the old one in with earth
And mark it with a stick.

Sometimes you'd forget your sen
When you'd filled the hole in wi a shovel
Cos' you'd forget to mark it with a stick
They'd soon be a right kerfuffle.

You could always tell if not by the smell
When somebody had redug a pit,
They'd be shouting from t'bushes, 'Bloody 'ell fire
I'm up to mi kneecaps in shit!'

Ee! I have to laugh when I think of it
It really caused many wrankles
With scout chasing scout and swingin' t'shovel
And with his trousers round his ankles.

If you were on cooking duty
There's one thing you had to learn
Never, never, leave the fire
Or let the cooking burn.

You had to counteract the smoke
The very best you could
To stop the food tasting of smoke
You put in a piece of wood.

So now that we were camping
And away from parents and 'digs'
We could go to t'shop at the end of the road
And buy ourselves some cigs.

So we'd go up to t'sweet shop in t'village
At the end of a road called t'long mile,
We'd buy a pack of five Woodbines
And tek em back to t'tent wi a smile.

You'd to sneak yer cigs in to t'tent though
If Skip knew they'd be a Hell of a row
Cos if you were caught smoking in those days
It was a major crime, not like now.

I often think of seeing a tent
Where all t'scouts would be inside smoking
They'd be clouds of smoke comin out thro door
And they'd be noises like coughin' and chokin'.

Now I didn't have much money
So I only had one or two
And I didn't really like 'em
But it was the thing to do.

I only puffed the smoke in
And blew it out again.
I was bad, I shouldn't be smoking
But at camp you could do anything then.

We had a lovely time at night
Before we went to bed
Singing songs round the camp fire
Whilst the sky was turning red.

We sang songs like 'Ging Gang Gooly'
And 'He's my brother – Sylvest'
And 'Rolling along on the crest of the wave'
If you'd have heard us, you'd have been impressed.

With crickets chirping and midges flying
With sun gone, it's getting cold
With tent zipped up; into sleeping bags
Then sleep, after ghost stories told.

I have many fond memories of camping
And the scouts and the pals that I had,
Of the smells and the feeling of well-being
All of them made me feel glad.

The field that I camped in with Barry
For our camping badge so long ago
Is still there today unaltered
I saw it in the last year or so.

I also drove past 'Squirrel Wood',
The smells of the nettles and trees
And 'the long mile' that led to the entrance
Helped bring back my memories.

CHAPTER SIXTEEN

OUR CHRISTMASES

Our Christmases were very good really
Compared to the rest of the year,
When apart from mi games and mi playing
There really wasn't much cheer.

Despite not having much money
And the fact that there wasn't much to buy
Mam and dad did the best they could really
And to get on they really did try.

Christmas for us kids started early
In a way like the kids of today
Except for them it starts on the telly,
For us it was in a different way.

For the kids of today they get blasted
With T.V. adverts from August and on
For expensive computers and robots
And dolls and games and so on.

But we never had advertising,
The excitement was all in our minds,
Of the thought of a 'chimney hung' stocking
Filled with goodies of all kinds.

The thought of getting a Dinky
Or a game or a red toy 'bus
Or some Smarties and a Mars Bar
Brought great excitement to us.

We started carol singing early
To earn a bob or so
But we didn't get much 'till Christmas Eve
There wern't much money you know.

But most people gave us a penny
For singing on Christmas night
So we'd have something to spend after Christmas
When mam and dad's 'purse' would be tight.

I particularly remember one Christmas,
We were singing at an old lady's door
We knocked and said, 'Merry Christmas'
When we'd finished our musical score.

The door opened and there stood a lady
She was old with a smile on her face,
'That was lovely,' she said, 'But I've got nowt
Will you have these mince pies in place?'

'I'm a pensioner you see,' said the lady,
'And I don't have much money to spare
But if you'll have these mince pies instead of cash
You'll know for your singing I care.'

So we took them and said 'Merry Christmas'
And thanked her for the mince pies,
She must have been quite sad and lonely
Cos she had some tears in her eyes.

Now I don't really know why I did it
Cos I'd never done it before
But we turned round and went back to see her
And again we knocked on her door.

She came to the door to see us
And asked if we were alright
And we gave her all of the money
We'd got for singing that night.

I can't really think why we did it
But we did, that's all I can say,
So we went home without any money
But ni mind it's nearly Christmas Day.

I'd wake up on Christmas morning
Sometimes at four o'clock
And I'd dash down stairs to t'fireplace
To check my hanging sock.

I'd check the table first of all
To see if Santa Claus
Had eaten those mince pies and buns
We'd left there for his cause.

I didn't get a lot of presents
But what I did was good
I'll be able to play with all mi toys
Before we have Christmas pud.

I always got an apple and an orange in mi sock
And I always got a penny that was new,
I'd get a Mars Selection Box with chocolate bars and such
And possibly a car in red or blue.

Our Christmas morning ritual
Was to take my toys next door
To show to mi best friend Baz
And they'd join his, on the floor.

Then home for Christmas dinner,
We'd have a piece of pork
With apple sauce and crackling
Dad carved with knife and fork.

We never had a turkey,
Just pork, but it was good
With sprouts and roast potatoes
Then custard and Christmas pud.

One thing you should remember
We'd enjoy our toys all day,
There was no such thing as Christmas telly
To distract us in any way.

Then when the day was over
I'd got to bed right good
It's been a lovely day, 'Thanks Santa
And thanks mam for mi Christmas pud.'

CHAPTER SEVENTEEN

MISCHIEF

Like children of all ages
We were right little devils at times
But as said in my earlier writings
Ours were relatively minor crimes.

The reason as stated was simple
You got thumped at home and at school,
You didn't swear, you weren't rude or destructive,
Discipline was the golden rule.

Nevertheless we were children
And if given half a chance
We would do things we knew that we shouldn't
Then suffer the circumstance.

Our favourite 'crime' was to ring doorbells
While playing out at night
We'd sneak up to a house and ring it
Then run and hide out of sight.

Now if your door had a doorbell
We always thought you were rich
And the wealth of people who lived there
Was dependent on the doorbell's pitch.

We'd ring bells at all sorts of houses,
Some had long drives, some had not,
The ones at the side of the footpath
Had bells much easier to spot.

The bells that we liked to hear best though
And we heard them many times
Were the bells on the 'poshest' houses,
Bells with Westminster Chimes.

It's funny to think that some houses
Where we rang bells at that time
Are blocks of stone terraces, they're not posh at all,
Even though they'd got Westminster Chimes.

We were also quite good at 'scrumping',
That means stealing apples today,
We'd size up the places where apple trees were
And make sure we'd remember the way.

We had to make sure that the apples and pears
Were a long way away from the house
So that people who lived there had no real idea
We were pinching the fruit from the boughs.

There was one time that sticks in my mind,
We were coming from Sunday School,
We were passing the gardens of Highfield Flats
And we fancied some fruit something cruel.

So we climbed over t'wall into t'orchard
I'd be dressed in my Sunday best
There were apples and pears all over the place
I was really very impressed.

We'd got one or two of the 'stolen' fruits
When suddenly I did espy
A beautiful pear of gigantic size
And to get it, I thought I would try.

It was high in the tree but climbing was out,
It was right at the end of a twig,
So we had to resort to a stone throw onslaught
We looked for some stones nice and big.

We were throwing for ages at the flippin' pear
But none of us had even got near
We couldn't stop much longer or else we'd get caught
And that would cost us quite dear.

'I'll have one more throw,' I said to mi pals,
'And then I'll 'ave to go.'
But Trevor, mi pal, was standing in front
And he'd decided to throw.

He raised his hand to throw the stone
His hand went behind his head
But instead of hitting the pear on the tree
He hit me on t'head instead.

He caught me on the forehead as his hand came back,
A pointed stone he was using,
The point of the stone stuck right in my head
And blood from the wound started oozing.

With hand on my face and blood running down
And a stone in my other hand
I just looked up and aimed and unleashed the stone
I hit the pear and it fell to the land.

'Wor am ah gonna tell mi mam?' I said,
'Wi mi shirt all covered in blood
She'll know that I've been up to mischief
Or certainly been up to no good.'

'I'll 'ave to think of summat
If I'm to survive this thing at all
So I'll tell her that I fell down
And banged mi head on a wall.'

So this is what I told mi mam
And mi pals all backed me up
So she changed mi shirt and washed mi face
And gave me some tea to sup.

The cut was not a big one
Not deep in any way
But now on my grown-up forehead
I've still got the scar today.

Another thing we used to do
Was throwing stones at windows,
We never threw big stones though,
Just small pebbles and cinders.

I suppose that we were cowards
In a way to put it right
Cos' we didn't throw our stones by day
But by the dark of night.

We only threw a tiny stone
At windows to be fair
It wasn't to try and break them
It was just to cause a scare.

We'd walk up to the garden gate
And have a look around
And when we knew no one was there
We'd pick a pebble off the ground.

We'd throw the pebble at the glass
And listen for the splat
We'd then high tail it down the street
In thirty seconds flat.

One night whilst walking down the street
Whilst going to the 'Guild' at church
John Battie my companion said,
'Let's for some pebbles search.'

'We'll see how many windows
We can splatter in one go.'
I said, 'Alright then kid we'll do it
But we'll have to run faster though.'

So both of us had pebbles
Several in each hand,
We stood about ten feet apart
And we surveyed the land.

There seemed to be no one about
So we both spun round and round
Then we released our deadly load
And listened for the sound.

The pebbles splattered on several panes
On windows here and there
When suddenly a voice from t'dark
'Eh, yer buggers, come 'ear.'

We ran like mad down the street
As fast as our legs would go
But an angry man was chasing us
And he wasn't going slow.

I don't think I've ever run so fast,
Oh dear, what have I done!
I'm afraid if this man catches me
It's curtains for you my son.

We were running fast down Sandygate
And John was well ahead,
The running feet were pursuing us
I've got to hide instead.

The man was quite a way away
And a bend came in the street
It meant that I'd be out of sight
For a second from the running feet.

I saw this low wall looming
It was about five foot tall
So I ran right fast up to it
And I dived straight over t'wall.

It was soft earth for my landing
So I lay there quiet and still,
The running feet got nearer
I was sweating and feeling quite chill.

I had to curb my breathing
So as not to make a row,
There was heavy panting near the wall
It looked like I'd had it now.

But the 'feet' went past my hiding place
And disappeared from sound
So I carefully peered over the top of the wall
As I got up from the ground.

My pursuer was still running
Then he disappeared from sight
Round a bend down Sandygate
But he'd given me a fright.

I waited for a minute
Then I cleared the wall
And landed on the pavement,
I didn't feel bad at all.

So I carried on my journey
Towards the chapel hall
I'd been so very lucky
That I had found that wall.

But I was to get a nasty shock
As I walked on down the street,
Cos' my pursuer was coming back again
And we were bound to meet.

So I just kept on walking
Acting nonchalantly
And he just carried on walking past
How lucky could I be?

But one day it was inevitable
That my luck would soon run out
Because of my throwing stones at glass
I was going to get a clout.

One day on the allotments
I decided to take aim
At a tree, a tub or a shed or two
And a greenhouse window pane.

I threw a stone and hit the glass
And a voice said loud and clear,
'Tha's brok my glass, young Darby,
Yer little sod, come 'ere.'

But I ran away, I didn't stop,
I was very scared and sad
I was very worried also
Cos' he might tell mi dad.

I went home very sheepishly
And I knew I'd made a blunder
Cos' me dad was waiting on the step
And his face was just like thunder.

'Ah know what tha's bin doin',
Tha's broken somedis glass
Cos' he's been here to tell mi,
I'm gonna tan thi arse'.

So I got meself a thumping
I was sent to bed for sure
And I shan't be throwing pebbles
At windows anymore.

I remember on mischief night
We always had some fun
Although we never did much harm
We'd play a trick and run.

Apart from throwing stones and things
We'd take off dustbin lids
And hide them so they couldn't be found
Cos' we were only kids.

We used to take off people's gates
And they would do their nut
Cos' we'd swap them with another gate
So they couldn't make 'em shut.

When I look back at the things we did
I know they were wrong in a way
But they were nothing at all to compare
With the things kids do today.

There weren't any car or bike thefts at all
No muggings or beating folks up,
No stealing of telly or video set
No torture of kitten or pup.

It was straightforward mischief, the things that kids do,
Without any malice or terror
Because there was fear and respect for the law
And to ignore this fact was an error.

CHAPTER EIGHTEEN

BONFIRE NIGHT

We always shared a bonfire wi t'neighbours,
In fact wi the neighbours next door,
We always had plenty of fireworks
Though all of us were really quite poor.

We never had it at our house
Mi dad didn't like it you see,
And he didn't want to spoil his garden
But nobody else seemed to worry.

We had all the usual goodies
That you have on bonfire night
Like toffee and parkin and taties
And chestnuts that tasted just right.

There were always plenty of kids there,
Our neighbours' relations of course,
They all brought lots of crackers
To add to the firework resource.

Mi mam always made some toffee
Though she'd never come and join in
She'd always go out or stay in the house,
She couldn't put up with the din.

Mi dad never joined in either
It's something he wasn't interested in
It's a good job our neighbours didn't mind mi coming
Otherwise I'd have to stop in.

We always handled fireworks
Not rockets but bangers and such
We used to throw them at lasses
But no one got hurt very much.

There was only one time when someone got hurt
And it happened to be yours truly,
It wasn't because we were acting daft
Or because we were being unruly.

It happened when a young lad called Melvyn,
A member of our neighbour's band,
Said, 'Put us this rocket in that bottle.'
And he gave it mi in mi hand.

I went to put it in't bottle
But there's one thing he'd forgotten to say
He forgot to tell me he'd lit it
And for that I was about to pay.

As I stooped down with the rocket
There was a hiss and a very loud woosh!
The rocket went off whilst still in mi hand
And mi fingers were turned to mush.

I cried out in pain, it was agony,
But nobody seemed to care
They got on with what they were doing
And I had to sit down in a chair.

I went in the house to see what I'd done
Mi fingers were a hell of a mess
The skin was all black and burnt to a crisp
And mi fingers a mass of bare flesh.

Nobody took me to the doctors
To the hospital or anywhere
Mi mam just put on a bandage
Nobody seemed to care.

'It's thi own stupid fault for handling things
Like rockets,' somebody said.
'If it had gone off much later than it actually did
It would have taken off top of thi head.'

I can remember the pain today
I just couldn't sleep that night
But mi mam never took me to Doctors or owt,
'In a few days tha'll be all right.'

All right I was no thanks to them,
I might easily 'ave lost mi fingers.
But the memory of our bonfire nights
In my mind well and truly lingers.

CHAPTER NINETEEN

THE PICTURES

I loved to go to the pictures
My mother would take me a lot,
Whether cowboys or tender love stories
Or thrillers with dastardly plots.

There were dozens of cinemas in those days
And they were nearly always full
We didn't have telly or video you see
But life was never dull.

We could go to the pictures for sixpence
Provided we sat at the front,
The front bit we called the 'chicken run'
It was a bit like that to be blunt.

You'd sit on the front row watching
And you'd be looking up at the screen
So your neck would have a permanent crick in it
When mam saw me she knew where I'd been.

Sometimes we would pay a bit extra
So we could sit at the back with the girls
We could snog or make them so angry
By sticking toffee in their curls.

Our 'pits' were the 'Grand' and 'Majestic',
They sound really posh I know,
But they weren't, they were really flea pits.
But it was exciting and we loved to go.

In those days there were a lot more 'heroes'
'Cowboys' you worshipped from afar
You could 'be them' when you were playing,
I can remember them all still nar.

There's Roy Rogers, Dale Evans and Trigger,
Gene Autrey and Champion his horse,
George Formby and Old Mother Riley,
Three Stooges and Tarzan of course.

We had Bud Abbot and Lou Costello,
Laurel and Hardy as well,
And Buster Grabbe played Flash Gordon,
All these stars were really swell.

We could watch Errol Flynn as the hero
As General Custer or Robin Hood,
He could be a ship's captain or pilot
He always played men that were 'good'.

Whenever you went to the pictures
An 'Usherette' showed you your seat,
She had a flashlight with a beam that showed up in the smoke
And a uniform all clean and neat.

If you were noisy or making a fuss
You'd be sure that she'd do her job,
She'd walk to your row, shine her torch in your face
And say to you, 'Eh, thee shut thi gob.'

The films of today aren't like they were then
There weren't any swearing or sex,
You didn't have full frontals or see any breasts
You didn't even see any 'kecks'.

Whenever the hero was kissing the girl
And it looked like he might 'get his way'
The camera would move away from the bed
And would come back 'later that day'.

And when t'cameras came back theyd be having a fag,
They'd blow smoke in each other's face,
But we knew just what they'd been doin'
Though her hair would be unruffled and in place.

There weren't many films in colour
They were mainly in black and white
But we didn't bother about colour or owt
As long as the excitement was right.

There was the Grand, Majestic and Cinema House,
Tivoli and Hippodrome too,
Electra, Classic and Regal Rawmarsh,
And Whitehall to name but a few.

There's the Royal, Premier and Empire,
The Odeon and Plaza as well,
The famous Rotherham Regent,
And Sheffield Lyceum so swell.

CHAPTER TWENTY

THE MATINEE

I will never forget Saturday Matinees,
In the morning together we'd go
For Roy Rogers, Dale Evans and Trigger,
Gene Autrey, Flash Gordon and Co.

There were Cartoons and Cowboys, Three Stooges an awl,
Flash Gordon and his enemy Ming,
We would cheer or we'd boo when they came on the screen
Ice cream cartons at the girls we would fling.

You could go to the matinee for threepence
And for a penny, ice cream in a carton,
The noise inside would be deafening
What with shoutin' and belchin' and fartin'.

Sometimes we got bored if the films weren't that good
So we'd crawl on the floor under seats,
The girls were our target most of the time
By removing the shoes from their feet.

However one day it came to an end
When enthusiasm did suddenly lack,
We could suddenly see we were crawling in pee
That had come from those sat at the back.

The Matinee Theatre is no longer there,
A supermarket stands there instead
But the memories of joy and fun that we had
Will live with me until I am dead.

When we came out of the Matinee
We would act the things that we'd seen
Whether Tarzan, Roy Rogers, Gene Autrey,
Or Flash Gordon and Ming so mean.

Now if we'd been watching a Cowboy
We would run like a horse in the street
With one hand stretched out holding reins
And the other hand slapping yer seat.

We'd make noises made by the cowboys
When they wanted their horses to go
And when we wanted to stop
We'd whinny and then we'd say 'whoa'.

My finger made a wonder pistol,
A Colt 45 or a Deringer,
Sometimes I would use both hands
If I were Roy Rogers or the Lone Ranger.

So you pointed your finger and made a loud bang
If you saw an Apache or Sioux,
It might be Brian or Baz or Trev,
But there was always a right todo.

You had to take turns being Indians
Cos' they were the ones that got shot
Even though they filled you with arrows
They were the ones that copped their lot.

I mean, how can you shoot Roy Rogers,
Or Dale Evans or Trigger his horse,
Or Gene Autrey with his Palamino 'Champion'?
If you did, you'd be full of remorse.

So if you were a Sioux or Apache
You'd be sure that the Cowboys would get yer
So you'd lay on the floor and you couldn't get up
Until somebody 'tigged' you better.

Now Molly Shaw was my sweetheart,
She lived in the house next door,
And she'd play at cowboys with us
She'd be on my side as well what's more.

I just had to be Roy Rogers
Even if I got shot
Cos with Molly to kiss me better
It did not matter a lot.

See! Roy Rogers was my hero
And Dale Evans was his wife,
So when I got shot by the Indians
She could kiss me back to life.

There'd be lads behind walls, lads behind trees,
All pointing their fingers and shooting,
There'd be other lads riding imaginary steeds
Playing at Indians and whooping.

Now if we'd been watching Tarzan
There'd be lots of little boys
Running home from the pictures
Making a Tarzan noise.

And if you could find a tree
With a branch that was low enough
You could jump up and swing with your arms or your legs
From the branch and do your Tarzan stuff.

The kids of today do just the same things
They play at the things they have seen
Whether it be on the telly or cinema too
Or on the video screen.

The big difference is that the films of today
Are full of violence and sex,
Of muggings and beatings and killing for fun,
There's no wonder their minds are such wrecks.

They haven't got the heroes we had in our films
Like Roy Rogers the 'Cowboy King',
Who'd kill all the bad guys then get on his horse
And pick up his guitar and sing.

I feel really sorry for the kids of today
Cos' I know just what they have missed
To have a hero who was kind but tough
And to see a lady simply 'kissed'.

It was the same with our comedy heroes,
Mother Riley and George Formby too,
Or Bud Abbott and Lou Costello,
Who never swore and were never blue.

You look at their films on the telly today
And you think that they are corny and daft
I suppose that they are compared with today
But they were very good at their craft.

George Formby to me was the best of the lot
With his songs and his ukelele
He would look straight ahead and smile whilst he sang
And I thought he was smiling at me.

With heroes like George and Roy Rogers
I suppose our minds were tuned in
To fun and simple excitement
Not to violence and musical 'din'.

So when you're watching your movies
Just remember when I was a lad
That I'd have more fun from my heroes
Than you'll ever have or have had.

CHAPTER TWENTY-ONE

SOME PASTIMES - WATH RACECOURSE

We had so many things to do in our lives
We never seemed to have a minute
Apart from games, we just 'did' things together,
Whether outside the house or in it.

The thing to remember in those times long past
Is that kids were generally safe
From being molested or kidnapped or killed
By a rapist or mugger or waif.

You could play anywhere in street or in field
Together or just on your own
But the days for letting your kids play out safe
Unfortunately and sadly are gone.

All you'd do was say to yer mam,
'Mam I'm going out to play.'
And she wouldn't even worry or give it a thought
That you'd be playing out somewhere all day.

It wasn't a case of neglect or ought
Or indifference to where you were at,
Cos nobody was any different
It was just natural and that was that.

We had a large area of grassland,
The old racecourse was its name,
It was away from houses and quite lonely too
We played for hours at many a game.

There was also a spinney, it was called 'Smithy Wood',
It was popular, with paths leading through
We'd spend time in there picking bluebells in spring
There were never any todo.

The racecourse and spinney were magic
For playing at cowboys and such
Cos it was soft when you fell, shot by Indians,
And therefore it didn't hurt very much.

Apart from playing at cowboys
You could be there on your own
And I used to go there with Molly
So we could spend some time alone.

We had a den on the racecourse
Hidden from strangers' eyes and sun
Where us lads and lasses spent hours together
In innocent laughter and fun.

Our best game was truth, dare or forfeit,
We had many a laugh playing it,
Us lads always wanted a forfeit
Or a dare; that was always a hit.

We used to take buns and bottles of pop
And bread and a few sticky sweets
We'd swop what we'd brought with each other
Even though they'd be mucky and 'un neat'.

I remember one day a relation of a pal
Came up from London to stay
She joined in our game but wanted to play
In the rude London way.

The dares and the forfeits were all very 'forward'
In fact they were all new to us,
We didn't know what some of the words meant that she said
It certainly caused a hell of a fuss.

She said that she thought we were backward
And spoilsports for not taking part
But the only thing I'll do in public, I said,
Is to swear, to belch or to fart.

Ee, I remember the racecourse with affection
You'd ger 'ome wi all tears in yer breeches
And yer 'ands and clothes and hair would be all mucky
It still fills mi mind with riches.

The favourite pastime I had
Was train spotting at Donny station
Where I'd go on Saturday mornings
With anyone, friend or relation.

I couldn't wait for Saturday morning
I'd get all excited and funny
So I'd go to bed early on Friday
I hope I shall have enough money.

CHAPTER TWENTY-TWO

THE TRAIN SPOTTER

At last it's Saturday morning
And I leap out from my bed,
No school, no chores, no homework,
I'm going train spotting instead.

The thought of seeing Mallard
Or any other streak
Has got me all excited
I've been like that all week.

I jump from my bed into trousers
To shoes and shirt and sock!
No time to stop for breakfast
T'train leaves at 9 o'clock.

'Tha not gooin wi aht the neck washed!'
Mi mam shouts from kitchen sink,
'And tha'd better get thi shoes cleaned
What will the neighbours think?'

But I don't care about neighbours
Or what my mam might say
There's more important things to do
On this 'train spotting' day.

Now, have I got mi train fare
My water and mi tuck?
And what is more important,
A pencil and train spotter's book?

So off I go with book in hand
And laces still untied
With one sock up and one sock down
And shirt lap hung outside.

I run down to the station
Not because I'm late
But because I might see smoke stacks
Steam and black footplate.

I'm catching t'train to 'Donny',
At 9 o'clock it goes
With Trevor, Baz and Brian,
They're mates a mine tha' knows.

I've now arrived at t'station,
Wath Central, platform 2,
And still it's only 8 o'clock
But I've got lots to do.

I buy a threepenny ticket
For 'Donny' there and back,
Now I'm on the platform
Flanking sleeper and double track.

We sit down for an hour
And watch the trains pass thro'
On't platform edge with dangling feet
Then t'bell rings loud and true.

We jump up quick and look down't track
Excited eyes eat distance,
From distant blob to steaming might
Comes conrod and clanking piston.

The mighty beast comes to a stop
And towers high above me,
The smell of steam, hot oil and smoke
Will never ever leave me.

I'm now on board as whistle blows
And jerking carriage moving
What joy, excitement, bliss and pride
I am every minute loving.

We arrive at 'Donny' station,
Can't wait to get off't train,
I must buy a platform ticket
Or I'll be sent back home again.

Oh how wonderful, how marvellous!
There's train and train and train
So I take out pen and 'spotter's' book,
It's great to be at 'Donny' again.

'Did tha see that?' Brian says
'That one sithee, look
It's 74632 'A' class.'
So I mark it in my book.

I've got no time for grub or drink
I'm far too excited and busy
I don't even know where I've put mi bag,
If mam knew she'd be right in a tizzy.

I've seen that one and I've seen that
But I've not seen that one before,
It's a namer yes! It's a namer!
It's 'Madame Pompadour'.

It's nearly 12 o'clock now
We are awaiting the London Express,
Will it or won't it be a 'streak'?
We argue and prattle and guess.

It's coming, it's coming, I can just see the front,
There's steam coming out of its side.
It's a 'streak', it's a 'streak' it's blue and it's black
It's 'Mallard' oh boy! What a sight.

It thunders on past and I stand there aghast,
I've never seen anything like it.
It was 'Mallard', yes, 'Mallard' my what a thrill!
At last from my book I can strike it.

It's getting near four, our train's coming in.
I suppose that we'd better make tracks
I don't want to go, I want to stay here,
But ni mind next week we'll be back.

'Yer back,' says mam, 'Have you had a good time?
You smell and you're covered in muck.'
'What do you think?' I say wiping grease from mi head
'I've seen "Mallard". Come and look at mi book.'

There are times in your life when you're lucky
To survive the things that you do
It happened to me train spotting
I was lucky I survived and grew.

The first time was on 'Donny' station,
We were standing at the side of the road,
That led to the goods yard from t'station
On the platform where they used to load.

I was talking to Trev, mi pal,
We were laughing and having some fun
I'd have told him a joke, nicked some of his grub,
We were laughing whatever I'd done.

He gave me a push with both hands on mi chest,
I know it was not intended,
But I lost my balance and started to fall
Something hard stopped me being upended.

I was hit by a car that was just passing by
At the same time Trevor had pushed,
I hit the car wing and fell on the ground
The driver must have been very flushed.

He screeched to a halt, jumped out of the car
And run up to where I was lying,
I was under the car with my legs sticking out
I bet the poor bloke started praying.

I'd just bumped my head and grazed all mi leg
But other than that I was fine.
He said, 'You daft bugger!' to Trevor
Who looked all pale and benign.

Nobody did owt about it
He just got in his car and drove off,
I might have had concussion
Or mi leg might have had to come off.

The second time that I was lucky
It happened at 'Donny' again,
I'd walked from the station to go to the sheds
Where they serviced and 'mended' the trains.

Now I've said earlier on in a chapter
That we didn't have perverts then,
But there had to be some, you can't say there weren't,
Even though they'd be an exception.

I was stood near a bridge trying to see
All the trains on the tracks below,
But I was far too small to see over the top
So I decided to get down and go.

Then a man in a cap and blue overalls
Came up - he was really quite tall -
'Does tha want to see trains?' he said with a smile,
'Come 'ere I'll sit thi on't wall.'

So he sat me down to look at the trains
They were scattered around willy nilly
Then suddenly he put his hand on my leg
And he started to play with mi willy.

I didn't like that so I jumped off the wall
But he said, 'I just wanted to see.
If tha comes in these toilets I'll just have a look
So come on lad, come in 'ere wi me.'

But I got really scared and then I ran off
Back to the station right quick
There's nobody going to take me in there
They're not going to look at my dick.

I suppose when I think, I was lucky,
At least I had the sense to run off
In today's world it might have been different
I might not have been so easily let off.

CHAPTER TWENTY-THREE

MORE PASTIMES
'WEMBLEY AND LORDS'

We had an area called Sycamore Crescent
Which was an area of rough grass and scrub
But to us it was all important
As our football and cricket club.

We'd play there on nights in the summer
And at weekends all the year round,
You would always see lots of activity
On our cricket and football ground.

We'd rush home from school, gulp down our tea
And dash to the 'Cres.' pretty fast,
Cos if you were late you wouldn't get picked
And if you did you'd be picked to bat last.

We had an oil drum for wickets at one end
And a wooden box at the other,
The bats weren't all that good either
And the ball was certainly not leather.

There were two lads who were always captain
And they were the ones that picked t'team.
'I'll have him, I'll have him,' etc. they'd say,
And the first to be picked was the cream.

I was always picked last at cricket
I can never understand why,
Just because I didn't know where to stand
Or because I couldn't catch the ball in the sky.

I was always poor at fielding,
I was always put far away
From the wickets and near to the boundary
And there for hours I'd stay.

They always let me play though,
Because I was part of the gang,
We were pals and all played together
The games always went off with a bang.

I remember though on one sunny evening
I was fielding at my usual place
When the batsman hit a ball towards me
At quite a remarkable pace.

The ball was reaching the boundary
Several feet to my right
It looked certain to be a six
But I had the ball in my sight.

I leapt to the right, caught the ball in mid-air
And fell on the floor with a puff,
A finer catch had never been seen
It was better than Harry Hough.

I got patted on t'back and patted on t'head
It was the only thing I'd ever done,
Cos I admit I was rubbish at cricket
But I'd saved another run.

It was a different story at football though,
I can say that here and nar,
And they didn't wait 'till last to pick me this time
Cos I was really a star.

Our goal posts were made of piled up coats
About five paces apart
And by t'time we'd finished they'd be in a right state
And only fit for a dust cart.

Now when I played football in t'Crescent
I was treated in a different seam
Because apart from being one of the best
I was a star in the school football team.

It was just like a player from Barnsley
Playing football with lads in the street,
I felt like Stanley Matthews
Dribbling with the ball at mi feet.

I didn't always play at goalie then,
I was a winger; I was fast and slick
They had a hell of a job to catch me,
And I scored many a hat trick.

But then I'd be the goalie again
I'd show 'em I knew my stuff
Cos apart from being Stan Matthews
I could also be Harry Hough.

We spent many nights and many days
Playing in Sycamore Crescent,
It was our 'Wembley' and 'Lords' rolled into one
It was my 'then', my 'past', my 'present'.

CHAPTER TWENTY-FOUR

THE KITE FLYERS

Another great pastime of ours
Was the making and flying of kites,
We could sit there for hours watching them fly
Whatever the location or sites.

The kites of today are all posh and refined,
They're shaped like birds and things,
Whereas the kites that we had were made from sticks
Brown paper, glue and string.

We would get some cane and form a cross
And tie it with string in the middle
Then tie some more around each point of the cross,
Sometimes it were a proper fiddle.

You'd then get some paper and tie it to t'cane
And glue it to the back as well,
Then you'd tie some string to each end of the cross
To tie your line to it so swell.

We made square ones too with a square cane frame
And a cross shape all tied together
When covered with paper and all painted up
You hoped it would fly in any weather.

You then made your 'tailings' from paper rolled up
And tied to some string every foot,
The kite was then ready to fly in the sky,
You hoped it would fly pretty good.

The length of the 'tailings' was a sign of prestige
Providing you could make the kite fly
So with line in hand and kite laid on t'floor
You'd run and have a good try.

A well designed kite would lift off the ground
And soar like a bird into space
You'd let out some line so the kite could take off
And you'd run with your string at great pace.

If the kite was no good for flying
You'd find out in a second or so
Cos the kite would go round in circles
Then plunge to the ground you know.

But if it took off and flew in the sky
You'd a wonderful feeling of pride
So you'd let out your line, as much as you'd got,
And just watch it, sat at the road side.

I could stand in my garden at home
And see dozens of kites in the sky,
All the kids were flying them in Sycamore Cres.
At least they were having a try.

There was always one kite that was highest,
It was just like a dot in the sky,
It was made by a kite-making genius
He could have made a table fly.

The man was retarded and didn't go to school
I just can't remember his name
But, boy oh boy, could he make a kite!
No one could make them the same.

They were aerodynamically perfect,
Always big with 'tailings' quite long,
They were made with precision and love
They'd stay up in winds high and strong.

He always had big balls of string
That would make the kites fly so high,
They would stay in the air with no movement
Like a permanent spot in the sky.

One twitch of his hand and the kite would respond
To left, to right, up or down,
It would take him an hour to wind it back in
And bring it back down to the ground.

The kids all loved him and admired his skill
And watched for hours his kite in the sky,
Choose how good our kites were they never matched his
No matter how hard we did try.

CHAPTER TWENTY-FIVE

CONKERS AND MARBLES

The next popular games of our era
Mainly at school but elsewhere
Were the games of marbles and conkers
And at both I suppose I was fair.

The King of Marbles and Conkers
Was Johnny Whitehouse, no less,
The lad that was always in trouble
But he was good at both, no mess.

When the conker season started
We would all go off to the woods
And collect as many horsechestnuts
And carry as many as we could.

We would take home all our treasures,
Remove them from their pods,
And select and grade the conkers
That would survive against the 'odds'.

You had to 'hole' the conker
As carefully as you could
Make sure you didn't crack the skin
Or weaken it you surely would.

When carefully holed you'd get your string
And feed it through the 'bore',
Knot the end then hold it up
And your conker was ready for war.

Now challengers were in earnest,
There were battles long and dour,
With conker smashing conker
And debris all over the floor.

Now when you smashed a conker
Belonging to one of your foes
You could add the score to your conker
So that its number quickly grows.

So if you had a 'tenner'
It meant you'd had ten wins
So it became a battle for 'champion'
And battle again begins.

If you smashed someone's conker
And he'd a 'twenty-four'
You could take that number from it
And add it to your score.

Eventually there'd be rumours
Going around the town
That he's got that and he's got that
And soon there'd be a showdown.

Then finally the challengers
Are stood there toe to toe,
The conkers hung there on their string
Ready to match blow for blow.

Now John had a secret method
Of making his conkers hard
So you could always be sure of his presence
At the showdown there in the yard.

The most popular game in the playground
Was marbles, without any doubt,
There'd always be plenty of games going on
And plenty of marbles about.

Now John was really the best player,
At least a better player than many,
He carried a bag full of marbles
And he sold them ten for a penny.

There were three games of marbles we played,
'Killer', 'Podge' and 'Chubs On',
They were mainly played in the playground
I was pretty good at every one.

For 'Killer' you drew a big circle
And you put your marbles inside,
As many as you wanted could play it
And you stood around the circle side.

The circle would be full of marbles
And when it was your turn
You threw another marble to try and knock some out
And any that you did you would earn.

The other game we played was 'Chubs On',
You didn't win so many at this game,
You could run a mile a day to win one marble
Then run another mile and do the same.

You only played this game with one more person
So you got someone who was boss-eyed or couldn't see,
Or someone who'd miss a barn door at two paces
So John would say, 'Aye up Malc. I'll play thee.'

150

If you went first you threw your marble onward
Then your partner threw his to follow yours,
And so on, until you hit your partner's marble
And when you did, then his marble became yours.

You could play 'Chubs On' while going to school in t'morning,
On the pavement, on the road, or passage way,
Then play it coming home again at teatime
Without hitting t'opponent's marble either way.

The favourite game of all was 'Podge' though,
You could win a lot of 'mabs.' at that,
It was played mainly in the playground
Where the surface of the yard was flat.

You would make a little hole in the pavement
Up against the playground wall
Then you'd roll as many marbles as you wanted
To get as many 'mabs.' as you could in the hole.

Your opponent would then do likewise
And the one who got the most inside the hole
Would take both sets of marbles together
And with both sets would have another roll.

Now when you rolled the marbles up together
You had to get one marble in the hole
When the others rolled away you could stop them
Then try and nudge them in and win them all.

You could have as many players as you wanted,
And play 'twos' or 'fours' or 'tens' up as you wish,
You can imagine with ten players playing 'tens up'
For the 'roll up' you'd need hands just like a dish.

The game of mabs. was played at school
As long as I was there,
It kept us out of mischief
And out of mother's hair.

I don't know whether marbles
Are played at school today
But the kids don't know what they're missing
If they don't play 'mabs.' each day.

CHAPTER TWENTY-SIX

THE BULLY

Every school has a bully,
We had one, not only at school,
We had one who used to come where we played
He was big and thick and a fool.

I can't remember what they called him,
'Froth' he was known as to us.
I remember he was tall with black curly hair
And to us he was really a cuss.

He'd pinch all your sweets, your bat or your ball,
He'd come and mow down your wickets,
But only if us little ones were playing alone
He couldn't stop big lads playing cricket.

You'd be playing all lovely, not making a fuss,
When owd Froth would creep up then yell,
Then he'd chase you and catch you and give you a clip
Sometimes you'd run away like hell.

You didn't like to pass him when you were alone
Cos he'd get you and give you a clout,
So you'd walk with great care when you passed his house
Just in case he was playing out.

Now my best pal was Bri Dyson
And he was smaller than me
But we were really inseparable,
We'd been mates since we were two you see.

We always seemed to be targets
For 'Froth' to have some fun,
But he couldn't give us a hiding
If we saw him first, cos we'd run.

But after a while Bri and me
Were getting fed up with him,
It's about time we stood up and gave him some stick
Otherwise our lives will always be grim.

'We're gooin' to 'ave to gerrim and gi' 'im some fist
Me and thee,' I said to Bri one day.
'If we do it together we've got a good chance
And if we 'ent we can soon run away.'

So we decided to get him and give him some smack
The next time he tries it with us,
He'll know what it's like to be smacked in the gob,
He'll think he's been hit by a bus.

Now there was an old air-raid shelter in Sycamore Crescent
Built of brick, with a door at each end,
It was filled with rubbish and used as a 'bog'
The smell inside you could not comprehend.

We were playing near here at football, I think,
Kicking the ball at the wall
When 'Froth' saw us playing he ran up to us
And said, 'Aye thee, gi mi that ball.'

'Get lost,' I said, or something like that,
'Tha not hitting us any more
And if tha tries it tha'll get some smack
And tha'll finish up on't floor.'

At this old 'Froth' were livid
And he came at us all angry and tough
But we managed to get him against the brick wall
And went in with fists, feet and stuff.

We didn't half give him a pasting
Although he gave us some too,
I bet he went home with a flea in his ear
And his legs and his arms black and blue.

Now 'Froth' never bothered us anymore
We could play without being bullied,
Whenever we saw him he'd swear and rant on
Looking all worried and sullied.

But he never attacked us again though,
Even if I was by mi sen,
Cos he knew that when I was wi Bri, mi pal
He'd get smacked in t'gob again.

So if ever you get thumped by a bully
And he makes you upset and depressed
Just do to him what he's done to you,
But do it together. He'll be impressed.

CHAPTER TWENTY-SEVEN

RATCATCHING

Now our neighbours who lived next door
Had a shed for the rabbits they kept,
On occasions I would go round and help them
On the day that the hutch was swept.

One day we saw a movement
And a hole underneath the hutch,
We knew it couldn't be a rabbit
Cos they didn't go under the shed much.

One day I saw in the garden
Something I thought was a cat
Until on further observation
When I noticed it was a huge rat.

It walked down the garden a while
Then, more movement under the shed,
And before you knew what was happening
Another one popped up his head.

I went to tell mi neighbour
Exactly what I had seen
And the two rats ran when they heard me
Back to the hole where they'd been.

The rats had caused such a commotion
They decided to have a rat hunt
So they got a man with a ferret,
A yellow vicious little runt.

We all stood round the shed watching
And the ferret was put down the hole,
Ken had a stick and a shovel
And I had a big lump of coal.

After a while we could hear squeaking and rustling
And rats emerged from their den,
There were lots of them running all over
Chased by boys and by men.

There was wielding of spades and pick handles
And clanging of spades on the ground,
Some of the rats were flattened
Others were no longer around.

I remember that Ken saw a beauty
Pop its head out of the hole
So he took a swipe with his shovel
And chopped the rat's head off whole.

I remember the rat expedition
Lasted a few days in all
Then we dug out and filled all the nests in,
I suppose we'd had quite a ball.

CHAPTER TWENTY-EIGHT

STREET GAMES

The games that we played were simple,
There were no fancy gadgets or toys,
We just played together as playmates
A mixture of girls and of boys.

We'd rush out to play straight after tea
And meet up by the gas lamp,
On Saturdays and Sundays when there was no school
In daylight or dark it was champ.

The kids of today do just the same things,
They meet their friends on street corners,
Trouble is they don't seem to have owt to do
Except cause trouble for t'local house owners.

I don't mean the things that we did as kids,
Throwin pebbles or changing round gates,
I mean robbery, and muggin and violence
Or owt else that they might think is great.

You see all these riots on t'telly
And assaults on pensioners and 'cops',
Why can't they just play at kick-can
Or buy the sens whips and tops?

You could play on your own or play in a gang,
Dependent on what game you would play,
Be it tiggy or kick-can or whip and top
Or hopscotch or hide-an-seek say.

At tiggy you all had to play in a group
And you all mingled round except one,
Then he had to catch and touch you
Then say 'Tha's been tigged, nar thar on'.

Then it was your turn to chase all the girls
And catch them and 'tigg' them the same.
You'd play it like this, 'till you'd all had enough
Then you'd play at another game.

Kick-can was popular and really good fun,
It was like hide-an-seek in a way,
All you needed was an old empty can
And plenty of kids to play.

In the middle of the road you'd place the old can
And then decide who was on,
The can would be kicked as far as was poss.
When you fetched it back the others were gone.

So you'd place the can on the spot where it was
And you went to search for the gang
And whilst you were looking for someone to find
They could come out and kick the can with a bang.

You couldn't seek them out unless the old can
Was firmly placed on the spot,
But when it was you'd go off again
Shouting 'Coming, ready or not.'

When you caught your 'prey' it was their turn for on
And so it was your turn to hide
And you'd play it like this 'till you'd had enough
Or 'till you went to where you reside.

Whip and top was the best game of all,
We'd play it for hours on end,
The best thing about it, you could play it alone
Or together with your friends.

You'd to buy a top, you could make a whip
From a piece of string and a stick,
Then you'd tie a knot in the end of the string
To make your top go round quick.

We always coloured the top with chalk
In stripes like a rainbow's hue,
Then winding the string around the top
To set it spinning true.

I can still remember the sight today
Seeing all us kids in the street
Bending down with whips in hand,
Whipping the tops so neat.

There was the constant sound of whiplash
As the string was whipped like a lash
And the contact of whip on spinning top
Just had to be done with panache.

You'd to strike the top just in the right place
If you wanted to keep it spinning,
You could watch someone's top stop, they'd whipped it wrong,
So you'd all be laughing and grinning.

When you think of the games we played in those days,
And these are only a few,
It makes you realise we filled all our time
We always had something to do.

We didn't have time to get bored
Or to think about mugging a poor sod
Or to think about vandalising somebody's house
Cos we also believed in God.

There were times though when we hit trouble
When making a din in the streets,
When a woman would come out wi her fist up
Shouting 'Bugger off, mi husbands on neets.'

Generally speaking though people didn't bother
Cos we had to have somewhere to play,
And we didn't have computers and fancy toys
Not like the kids do today.

This is why it's surprising to me
Why kids cause such trouble today
When they've so much and so many things
They could stop in all day and play.

It shows we were more clever, dunt it,
And that todays kids can't think like us either,
Cos' we improvised and invented our pastimes
And it didn't cost us owt neither.

So come on, all you muggers and vandals,
Go and get an old can from your bin
And get your pals and play kick-can,
You won't have the time to commit sin.

THE FORTIES SKATEBOARDERS

I used to be good at skating,
Roller skates though, not on t'ice,
We only used one skate though
For two skates we couldn't afford t'price.

We didn't go skating though, stood on our feet
All posh like the Champions will,
You sat on yer bum, on a board, on a skate,
And skateboard like that, down a hill.

All you'd to do was wait for Christmas
Or a birthday of one of your 'rich' mates,
Then ask him to ask for skates as a present
Then you could borrow one of his skates.

If any kid was skating proper
Stood up wi two skates on his feet
We always said they were posh and rich
Even though they only lived in't next street.

We'd get our skate and find a board,
An old piece of floorboard was enough,
Then we'd go up to top of t'hill on Oak Road
Cos' it was steep and t'pavements weren't rough.

Ee! it looked just like t'start of a proper race,
Wi all t'kids stood there in rows,
Waiting for their turn to skate back down t'hill
Ee! It'll soon be mi turn tha knows.

When yer turn came yer put yer skate down
And yer put yer board on top,
It had to be balanced and central on't skate
Or else you'd fall off and stop.

Then yer sat on yer board wi yer legs stretched out
In front and stuck up in t'air,
Yer feet mustn't touch t'pavement or they'd slow yer down
And scraping feet yer speed would impair.

Yer held onto t'board wi one hand each side
Hand on top wi fingers below,
That were yer method of steering
Whether travelling fast or slow.

Press down wi yer left hand, the skate would turn left,
Press down wi yer right, to turn right,
Many's the time you'd scrape yer fingers on t'ground
That would then stop yer sleeping at night.

We always skated on t'pavement though,
Cos t'road surface was pebbles right rough,
And in summer when all the tar melted
You'd go home covered in tar and stuff.

And when yer got home, yer earoles were pounded
By yer mam. 'As tha seen thissen?
That covered in tar and just look at thi shoes,
And thi breeches arse is 'angin' aht agen.'

So yer stayed on t'pavement as much as yer could
They were stone slabs with joints and cracks,
Ee it were great, when yer wheels went over joints,
Cos' it sounded like train wheels over joints on't tracks.

Many's the time you'd be skating down t'road
And you'd hit a paving slab edge
And you'd fly off t'skate wi t'board anawl,
Trapping fingers under t'board like a wedge.

Now if anybody was walking on t'pavement
You'd to dodge an weave on your skate
And sometimes you'd to take drastic action
And finish up in somebody's hedge or gate.

I remember one time of distinction
On a crossing over t'footpath
Where a lorry were crossing to t'builders' yard
It said, 'Smickersgills, Builders of Wath.'

It was crossing the pavement, it was stood in fact,
The gap between t'wheels were quite wide
So wi didn't bother stopping, wi went underneath
And came back out at t'other side.

I remember these things so clearly,
We must have walked miles every day,
Cos you'd skate down t'hill hundreds of times
But you'd to walk back up t'hill the same way.

CHAPTER TWENTY-NINE

PARTY GAMES

Oh boy, did we have a time
At birthday parties and such,
Kissing and cuddling the girls all night,
The food didn't mean very much.

We all had birthday parties
They were the highlight of the year,
With cake and buns and jelly
Kissing and cuddling and cheer.

I only had one birthday party
My mam didn't like them you see,
But my mates always had plenty
And they still invited me.

You didn't choose your guests yourself though,
You chose them along with your mates,
Depending on which girl you fancied
For snogging and making a date.

We always invited Brenda
And Mavis and Maureen anawl,
They knew how to do French kissing
And didn't mind the odd grope at all.

As long as they didn't mind snogging
And weren't bossy and didn't moan or nag
They could be ugly wi a face like a bulldog,
You could cover their head wi a bag.

You could choose the girl that you wanted to come
Even though the host might not know her
Providing she liked a good snog and all that,
And didn't mind snogging on't floor.

We played some great party games at our parties
Like 'Winky' and spinning the plate,
'Postman's Knock' and 'Hyde Park Corner',
And any other we could create.

We always started our parties
With a 'nosh-up' when we arrived
At the table, all posh, with a cloth on,
With all the best that the mams could provide.

We always had potted meat sandwiches,
Always! and some wi fish paste,
And trifle blancmange and red jelly,
You never saw much waste.

We had homemade buns wi icing
With hundreds and thousands on top,
And butterfly buns wi cream in,
Ee! you didn't know when to stop.

We always had tinned peaches wi custard
Or tinned pears, just one or the other,
And sometimes you'd have real bananas
Mixed wi custard, made by yer mother.

You've got to remember in these times long past
That these things we had were a treat,
You only had em at parties,
No other time. Ee! it were neat.

We always started at tea-time,
We never started too late,
Cos' to lose any time for 'snogging'
We just could not contemplate.

Came the time for the 'action',
So you'd practise 'flexing' your lips,
With girl sat on knee in an armchair
With your arms round her waist or her hips.

'Spinning Plate' was the game we played first
Because it was really quite hectic,
You were up and down all the time
With the 'nosh' your stomach felt peptic.

Now when you spun the plate you called out the name
Of a girl and you'd look at her grinning,
She'd to rise from her seat and dash for the plate
And catch it before it stopped spinning.

If she caught it in time then she'd have a spin
And she'd call a lad's name out,
But if she didn't catch it before it had stopped
You got a kiss, so her lips she could pout.

If you called out the name of a girl you didn't fancy
You'd give the plate a big spin
But if you wanted a kiss from a girl that you liked
You'd stamp on the plate with a grin.

Now 'Winky' I suppose was quite similar,
Cos' you had a girl on your knee
Whilst the lad in the middle tried to get her to leave
By 'winking' so only she could see.

Now if you saw him winking
She'd try to leave your knee,
And if she made it he'd get a big kiss
Then he'd take your seat you see.

But you could stop her leaving
She might not want to try,
So you'd throw your arms around her waist
When your 'enemy' winked his eye.

'Hyde Park Corner' was the game,
It was one continuous snog,
You didn't have time for anything else
Not even a trip to the bog.

You had a girl upon your knee
An easy chair was better
The lights were out, so with some luck,
You could put your hand up her sweater.

Now whoever was 'on' would have a torch
And all round the room he'd walk,
Shining the torch on couples
You'd to kiss and couldn't talk.

We always felt really sorry
For the lad who was first with the light,
Cos' he could never catch you not snogging
He could have been shining the torch all night.

Now when we played 'Hyde Park Corner'
It would last for the rest of the night,
It was just an excuse for snogging
And we certainly snogged alright.

I should really say here and now though
That it was only snogging we did,
There was never any knickers flying
And nobody went on the bed.

It was always innocent snogging
We always had a lot of fun,
Well that's why you have parties, intit,
When all is said and done?

CHAPTER THIRTY

PRIVATE GAMES

Now I had a bike, a three wheeler type,
An old one for just a short while,
I'd ride it for hours playing alone
Round our streets for mile upon mile.

It was only an old one, it didn't last too long,
But while it did I could ride without fuss
Making mouth sounds just like an engine
Cos I had wheels now just like a bus.

I were ever so lucky to get it,
I were in t'right place at t'right time,
It only happens like that on occasions
But you have to have some luck sometime.

It were t'day for emptying t'dustbin,
They were out on t'pavement already,
When a man walked to his wi a three wheeler bike,
Ee! I just stood there an went all heady.

There weren't one inch e t'bike that weren't rusty
And t'wheels didn't go round very well,
There were no mudguards and some spokes were missin',
There were no tyres on t'wheels, and no bell.

'What tha dooin wi that bike, dunt tha want it?'
I said to the man with a grin.
'I dunt,' he said, 'it's stood outside ten years
And its 'ad it so its gooin in t'bin.'

'I'll 'ave it if tha dunt want it
Cos' I ent gor a bike tha sees.'
'What's tha want this for, it's buggered?' he said.
'Awe go on let me ave mister, please!'

So, he gave mi t'bike and I took it home
And mi dad said, 'Bugger me!
Wheer the 'ells that got that from?'
'I've had it gid dad so it's mine nar you see!'

So I took it on t'street to ride it,
You've never heard a bike mek such noise!
Wi rattlin et wheels and no tyres
But I rode it wi elegance and poise.

'I'll tell thi summat,' mi dad said, when he heard it,
'Even though thy ent gorra bell
They'll 'ear thi comin in Barnsley,
And they'll all run away like 'ell.'

I'd be riding along being a bus
Stopping at lamp-post and gate
Cos' these were my own private bus stops
Where imaginary passengers would wait.

Everyone knew my 'bus service',
They'd laugh when I went riding by,
'Is 'ere agean, sithee ger aht e way
Else tha'll finish on't floor an tha'll die.'

My favourite place for taking mi 'bus
Was to Riley Road at the end
Cos there was always a great big puddle
When it rained and great 'sprays' I would send.

171

I would ride through this puddle for hours on end
With mi feet splayed out at the sides
But the spray would still wet me thro' though,
During my water-splash rides.

I'd go home for tea with mi hair dripping wet
And mi bike all rusty and horrid.
'Tha's bin ridin' in't puddles agean,' mam would say
Making my life very torrid.

There's no wonder mi bike didn't last very long
Although it wasn't due to the dust
It was already old when I got it
And it dropped to bits with rust.

It's funny that forty years later
When fetching my father to stay
I'd drive my car in the very same puddle
That's in the same place still today.

I can remember with such great nostalgia
It makes me feel sad in a way
To think that my days of being a bus
Are now so far, far away.

It wouldn't be right now I'm a man,
In fact it would cause quite a fuss
To my wife and two gorgeous daughters
If I still played at being a bus!

Going to bed on a warm summer's night
Never filled me with dread
Because there were buses to play at,
The type that were played best in bed.

I can remember so clearly the warm summer nights
With the sun going down in the sky
And blue turning black and the twinkle of stars
As they came out for the night so high.

I would kneel on the floor with elbows on sill
And chin on hands, looking out,
Through open window with 'sash' raised up
And eyes 'scanning' round and about.

The noises I heard and the things I could see
Will live with me all of my days
For there's nothing like sound, sight or smell
To bring back our memories.

I remember the noise in the distance
Of steam and clanging and thump,
Of engines and waggons shunting
At the train yard down at 'Wath Hump'.

There'd be steam noise from engine funnel
And clanging of chains on release
And the thumping of 'contacting' waggons,
Noisy, shattering the peace.

And in the night sky in the distance
The glow of flame and fire
Lighting the sky incandescent
In the sky moving higher and higher.

The flames had been there forever
From coke ovens at Manvers Main
But now they have gone, not to return,
And the 'glow' won't be seen again.

I walked on the racecourse a few months ago,
My first time in forty odd years,
And the view that I saw was now different
And my eyes welled up with tears.

There is no winding gear, no hopper, no shed,
No coke ovens belching out smoke,
No stock piles of coal, no conveyors,
And no work for the local menfolk.

And although it is now open country
I'm sure I could see all the ghosts
Of miners, and silhouettes of buildings
And the ghost of my father the most.

The viewing of night however
Only came prior to going to sleep,
But before getting my head down
A date with my buses I'd keep.

I'd take off my sheet and the pillows
And smooth out the sheet on the bed,
For the bed was no longer for sleeping
It was a town and a garage instead.

A town and a garage needs buses
So I'd go to where Ken used to sleep
And borrow a number of hard backed books
Then back to my bedroom I'd creep.

The books would be my buses
Be they red or blue or brown
So long as they had a smooth cover
And were easy to push around.

But buses don't know where they're going
Unless it tells you so,
In its little glass frame with the 'place' written in
Saying where it's to go.

My buses would be no exception
They'd show where they're going to
So I'd write on the edge of the book's page
In crayon in red or in blue.

I remember the bus route numbers,
Twenty-three and twenty-three A,
Twenty-two and buses marked 'Woodman'
Some routes that aren't run today.

My buses would have all these numbers
And destinations written all neat
The bed would be full of buses,
In fact I'd have quite a fleet.

The buses were ready for working
So round the bed they would go,
Pushed by left hand and right hand
Moving fast and slow.

A bus is no good without passengers
So I made some from paper and card
Cut into little pieces,
A bus's life is so hard.

I'd have hundreds of pieces of paper
Scattered all over the bed
In groups stood at bus stops
Or some on the buses instead.

The noises of the engines and conductors' bells
Could be heard all over the site
Until it was time to lie down to sleep
And garage the buses. Goodnight.

A few years ago, I was having a clear out
Of drawers and wardrobes and such,
Of dad, who still lived in the same house as then,
But didn't have very much.

I was clearing out a drawer when to my delight
I found an old book – it was red,
But it wasn't a book really
It was a bus, the type used in bed.

It had twenty-three A written in front
And Doncaster-Barnsley too,
And 'paper' passengers inside the front leaf
Put there so long, long ago.

I now wished that I had kept that book
Of memories of private joy
But I dumped it along with the other stuff,
My memories of being a boy.

On long winter nights the buses would stop
It was too cold to play on the bed,
So I invented a game of patience
I could play in bed instead.

It was a game at football patience
Played with playing cards,
I played it for hours and hours
The rules weren't very hard.

And now forty years later
I still play the game today
Perfected after years of playing
It still gives me pleasure to play.

I've kept all my records and tables
Of cups and championships won
By Hearts, Spades, Clubs and Diamonds
It really has been great fun.

So as I look back on my childhood
And my own private games I did play
They obviously gave me great pleasure
And the memories are with me today.

CHAPTER THIRTY-ONE

BIOLOGY

We never did biology at school
We didn't even know what it meant,
We never learnt about bodies or owt
Or sex or sexual intent.

The kids of today are more 'forward'
And aware of their bodies and like
I were more interested in playing cowboys
Or riding on somebody's bike.

At 10 or 11 the kids of today
Are capable and ready for sex,
We didn't know what it was all about
Even if we saw lasses' kexs.

We used to laugh if we saw t'girls knickers,
Navy blue wi elastic round thighs,
They'd do P.T. with their skirts tucked int top
Ee! It were a right sight for sore eyes.

We'd watch 'em doing games int playground
And we'd guffaw and mock and shout,
Then t'teacher would grab yer by t'earole
And give you some stick or a clout.

It was nothing to do with sex, though,
It was innocent teasing and stuff
Just to let the girls know their places,
Just to show 'em that lads are tough.

At 10 I'd never seen ladies' privates
I thought they were t'same as mine,
But one day I was to learn the difference
For now, though, playing football will do fine.

I remember a girl called Maureen
Who would give me my first big thrill
She'd prove that we were both made different
Ee! I remember it with laughter now still.

One day in the street I saw Maureen
Wi mi pals all mingling around,
They'd run away one by one laughing
And I wondered just what they had found.

I asked mi pal, 'Eyop what tha doin'?'
'Ee, it's great,' he said, 'come and see,
If tha gives owd Maureen an aniseed ball
She'll drop em so tha can see.'

But I couldn't afford an aniseed ball
I'd only one left in mi bag
But if I don't have a look they'll laugh at mi
And they'll make mi life a drag.

So I decided to do some bartering instead
And I said to Maureen real fine,
'If tha lets me look for nowt Maureen
I'll let thi look at mine.'

So we swapped looks and ran away laughing
Acting all daft and silly
And I shouted, 'I've seen thi "thing" Maureen!'
And she said, 'I, and I've seen thy willy.'

But it was totally innocent playing
It just didn't mean owt to us
We'd forget it and carry on playing
Today though there'd be a hell of a fuss.

So that was the first time I realised
That girls were different to me
And I shrugged and thought I'd rather play Football
Than pay an aniseed ball just to see.

CHAPTER THIRTY-TWO

PRIVATE 'LORDS' AND 'WEMBLEY'

If I had a pound for each hour
I'd played cricket and football with Dave
I'd be wealthy and early retired
And wouldn't still need to save.

Dave Harrison was my neighbour
He was two years younger than me,
He was just as mad on cricket
And football as I was you see.

We'd play together every spare minute,
No matter how cold or how wet,
We'd even play football at night in the dark
For as much time as we could get.

Our 'Lords' cricket ground was the passage
That led between their house and ours
With 'chalk' wickets on't fence at the bottom
That would be bowled at for hours and hours.

It was quite common at holiday and weekends
For us to play cricket all day,
Just the two of us playing a test match
With commentary as well by the way.

We'd be commentating every minute
I'd mek cheering noises wi mi throat,
'It's Compton bowling to Bradman
'Ees aht L.B.W. for nought.'

We'd jump up and down like idiots
If England had won the test,
Even if Dave was Australia
Our cricket games were magic, the best.

Our bat was old and decrepit
With all the use it had had
And we played with a soft ball in rubber
Not a cricket ball – we weren't mad.

We never bowled 'over' we bowled underhand
You could still ball fast though, with spin,
And as soon as you saw some chalk fly
You'd shout 'owzatt' with a grin.

We had our own rules for scoring of runs
You didn't have to run at all,
You could stand there and play the most wonderful shots
And get a run for just hitting the ball.

You got four for hitting a 'screamer'
Past the bowler and hitting the gate
And if you bashed one past him and into the street
You got six; it would make you feel great.

I must tell you that the passage ceiling
Was supposed to be plaster and lath
But there was never any plaster on it,
Our cricketing saw to that.

Whenever you hit a ball in the air
It would hit the ceiling with pace
And the plaster and dust would come falling down
And cover your hair and face.

You could see through the laths to the floorboards
Of the bedrooms that were sited above
There was wiring and nails and cobwebs
And hanging plaster ready to move.

I suppose that our parents got fed up
With all the din and the noise,
But how could you be Dennis Compton
If you didn't have skill and poise?

I remember on several occasions
When dad had been working t'night shift
We'd be makin a noise playin cricket
So there was bound to be a rift.

He'd be in bed, we'd be at Lords,
There'd be commentary, excitement and din,
There'd be plaster flying as ball hit ceiling
We'd be oblivious to the danger within.

Then all of a sudden dad would appear,
Pyjamad and hair stood on end,
And teeth still in t'glass by the bedside
And our earoles with verbals he'd bend.

So we had to stop playing cricket
'Eyop Dave, we'll play football instead.'
So we'd take the same ball out to 'Wembley'
And play football while mi dad were in bed.

Now in the football season
We had our own Wembley so swell
The street with its raised-up pavements
And walls and hedges as well.

Our goals were the gate to our passage
And the gates to the Stacey's abode,
We were on one side with gates in a wall
Theirs were on the opposite side of the road.

The trouble with the goals at Stacey's
There were hedges to posts at each side
With big holes in that caused you problems
When the ball missed t'goals and went wide.

We played with a tennis ball or similar,
You needed great skill and panache,
To get the ball past raised pavements
And score a goal with a dash.

The ball kept going in Stacey's
The missus didn't like it at all
'Tha's 'ad it nar,' she said after fiftieth time,
'Tha can't cum agean for thi ball.'

But we were not to be beaten
We'd plenty of balls you see
But eventually she had a lawn full
Kicked there by David and me.

There must have been twenty at one time
Just there, lying about,
She never bothered to move them
So we waited until she went out.

As soon as she'd gone we fetched the balls out
And carried on with our game
When she came back she must have known
That we'd been in the garden again.

We'd play hours and hours and hours
The games were quite serious ones
I always had to be Barnsley
Dave said, 'Tha can be who tha wants.'

We must have gone through shoes like crazy
With kicking and scraping of feet
Mi mam was always saying
'Does tha think we find money in't street?'

And t'ceiling were never replastered
In fact there were no plaster at all
That's why my bedroom were full of draughts
But I'll tell yer we had a ball.

I remember these games with affection
We'd play innocently day after day
And David was as keen as I was
And as skilful in every way.

CHAPTER THIRTY-THREE

WATH BATHS

We had a swimming pool down in Wath
It wasn't very big but no matter
It didn't have proper changing rooms
It had cabins all round t'watter.

The girls changed at one side, the boys at the other,
With just the main entrance between
We would stand on our seats while changing to swim
To see over the top and be seen.

We'd shout rude remarks and throw things at the girls
Who'd be getting changed in the cabin,
Then we'd wait 'till they came out in cossy and hat
And chase them, nippin' and grabbin'.

The only thing wrong with having the cabins
Actually at the side of the pool
Your pals would run by and open your door
So the girls could see your bum and your 'tool'.

You always went home with your clothes wet
And your shoes full of water as well
Cos' you'd splash and throw water over the door,
If you knew who it was you didn't tell.

I never cared much for swimming
I wasn't very good at it you see
And because I was only quite little
The big boys would always duck me.

There's one thing I must say I did love
It was held on a Wednesday night,
Water Polo, you could get in for three pence
It was a smashing sport alright.

They'd put staging up over the cabins
So people could sit down and see
It was always full as I remember
Lots more liked it besides me.

There was always keen competition
It was league status and all done right
You could go and cheer on your heroes
And have a really good night.

They'd start off with swimming races,
Individual and relays for points,
Then they'd wind down the goal posts from t'ceiling
And secure them in place with joints.

The teams would dive in ready to start
They had on little skull caps
Wath's were red and white striped ones
Tied under the chin with straps.

Water Polo is very exciting,
Swimming and pushing the ball,
Then picking the ball up and shooting
And trying to score a goal.

The noise in the baths would be deafening
You can imagine with cheering and all
And the noise of splashing and swimming
And the thud as ball hit the wall.

It was good though, I really enjoyed it,
It was another part of my life
That had been both exciting and varied
And sometimes with a little strife.

CHAPTER THIRTY-FOUR

THE SOUNDS AND SMELLS OF MEMORY

I'd to take the eleven plus exam
It was compulsory then in that day
But I failed it; I weren't really bothered,
Cos at Park Road wi mi mates I could stay.

None of mi pals passed either
But suddenly I thought there and then
I won't be able to go into the R.A.F. now
And fly Lancasters and Jets like Ken.

Ni mind though, there'll be another chance later,
But if not I'll be a draughtsman instead
So I'll stay wi Bri at Park Road School
It didn't fill me with dread.

There weren't much happening at 11 and 12
Except what I've already said
But there's nothing like sounds and smells in your nose
To bring memories into your head.

As I've said we played on the racecourse
But to get there there was only one way
We had to go through the allotments
Where gardeners spent most of the day.

I remember the cart tracks, mainly of sand,
With deep gullies caused by the rain
Where the rainwater ran as it had done for years
Until it reached the rainwater drain.

There were muck heaps with dried hops from the brewery in Wath
They had a most distinctive smell
Everyone had them to use as manure
Mixed with horse muck as well.

There were rickety fences and home-made gates
And the smell of creosote and tar,
There were dozens of pigeon lofts scattered about
Where the birds would fly to from afar.

I remember the rhubarb and cabbage plants too
And the nobbly stemmed brussel sprout plants,
The smell of the leaves where they'd rotted
And the caterpillar, black snails and ants.

We had to pass by Miller's wood-yard
I remember the noise and the smell,
The dust coming out from the dark of the shed
And the piles of sawdust as well.

I can hear the noise of the steam engine
Driving the pulley, 'phut, phut, phut',
And the slap of the belt as it went round and round
Driving the circular saw in the hut.

I remember old man Miller
With his droopy moustache and a smile,
His trouser-legs tied at the knees with some string
There was more dust on him than on't pile.

Things like this though you never forget
They stay in your mind for good
And you know that you can never 'ave 'em back
But sometimes you wish that you could.

FISH & CHIPS AND ICE CREAM

I remember the smell of our Chip Shop,
They were lovely, the best ones around,
From a small wooden hut in Sandygate Road
Better Fish and Chips just couldn't be found.

You didn't get much for your money
But what you did get was really right great
They were noted for small fish and not many chips
You didn't get a lot on your plate.

Elliott's was the name of the Chip Shop
And Doris was employed there to serve,
She had straggly hair and wore pumps on her feet
And she had no passion or verve.

She was really quite dozey and talked very slow
She slouched and said, 'What does tha want?'
'A penneth of chips and some fish bits,' I'd say.
'Is that all?' she'd say with a grunt.

It took her ages to serve you
Her movements were terribly slow
The queue could be out on the pavement
It made no difference though.

Now Mrs Elliott, the owner,
Would watch while Doris served chips
She'd shout at yer if yer made a noise
Stood with her hands on her hips.

We never had chips in a bag or ought
They were just in newspaper, that's all,
But boy they were lovely, I can taste them now
Newspaper print anawl.

I also remember the ice cream we had,
Massarella's it was in that day,
He'd just started his Ice Cream Empire
That's made him wealthy today.

When the van came with ice cream in those days
They didn't have bells they'd just shout
They'd pull up and just shout 'Ice Cream'
Hoping that kids would come out.

We could buy a cornet for a penny
Or for threepence a sandwich or tub,
There was only plain ice cream, not like today
But the ice cream was 'loverly grub.'

We had a girl in our street
Who couldn't sound her words at all
She'd ask for a 'Tenny Tornet'
'Here's Tenny Torniter,' we'd call.

Ee! I'll never forget Elliott's Chip Shop,
Or Massarella's Ice Cream van too,
I still lick my lips when I think of the taste
And all t'queueing for 'em that wi used to do.

CHAPTER THIRTY-FIVE

A DREAM COME TRUE

We all have our dreams whatever they are
Be it money or fortune or like
But I had a dream, I'd had it for years,
I wanted a two wheeler bike.

But I had another dream also,
I'd had that for years too you see,
I vowed one day that I'd visit my Ken
Seeing as he could not come and see me.

Thanks to my mam doing work at the school
And my time cleaning windows too
Plus being errand boy working for the man at the shop
My dream was about to come true.

'Tha's done right well passing for't Tech,'
Mi mam said as proud as can be,
'So I'm tekin thi to Wombwell to t'bike shop
To see what bikes we can see.'

So we went to Diggles bike shop
And I can still remember today
When we opened the doors I remember the smell
Of tyres and oil and paint spray.

There were dozens of bikes all lined up in rows
On stands to hold the bikes up
They were shining and glistening and their paint was all new,
I was gob-smacked, excited, full up.

Now I knew we couldn't afford a posh one
With aluminium wheels and frame
They were so light you could lift them up with one hand
But they were only a bike just the same.

Then I saw it stood there all neat in its row,
The bike that I'd ask mam to buy,
It was turquoise and silver with drop handlebars
'Oo mam, if I can't have that one I'll die.'

'How much is that one?' she said to the man,
'That one in Kingfisher blue,'
'It's ten shillings down and five bob a week
For two years.' 'Good,' said mam, 'That'll do.'

The bike was a Phillip's Kingfisher
It had Kingfisher written down t'frame,
It had lights and a bell and bottles on't front,
My life won't be the same again.

'We'll deliver on Thursday if that's alright,'
Mr Diggles said feeling right chuffed.
'We don't want it sending, I'm riding it 'ome,'
I said to Mr Diggles. He felt sloughed.

'That's alright,' said mam, 'I'll go 'ome on't 'bus
Our Mally will go 'ome on 'is bike.
So ah'l si thi later, don't do owt daft
Like pedalling too fast en't like.'

So mam caught a 'bus to go home to Wath
And left me alone it would seem
I just couldn't believe it I stood there aghast
Looking at my realised dream.

I leaned my bike up for a minute or two
Watching it gleam in the sun
It was mine, all mine, I could go where I wanted
Well done, Malcolm, my son.

EPILOGUE

It's only now when I have been able to delve into my memory that I realise just what an active early childhood I had. I wonder now how I managed to fit in everything that I did. Of course over a nine year period there are a lot of days and a lot of hours to fill but I obviously managed to fill them.

It was never a case of being bored or waiting to see what was on T.V. next. No sitting twiddling thumbs or wondering what the heck to do with yourself.

Whether with a gang or on my own I realise now just how I enjoyed myself.

Of course in this day and age restrictions are greater in terms of children being free and safe to play alone or away from home. In our day I just do not even think it was thought of that we would be abducted or worse.

It was rare in those days for mam or dad to say, 'Don't go too far away.' We could play miles away without any bother.

However, 'Don't thee be 'ome late lad' meant don't be home late because early bed times were the norm, not because parents were worried about you being out late due to any of the pre-mentioned dangers.

Playing out at night in those days was quite normal. You had to, there was nothing else to do. No T.V. no video. No music centres, only radio and then at night, no children's programmes. We had very few books and couldn't afford any, so you played with your friends at games that were nearly always free.

I was fortunate to have quite an inventive mind and an active mind too. My 'Bed Type Buses' and 'Card Games' are evidence of that.

I was fortunate also to live in a time when kids didn't have too many things to occupy their minds, because we didn't have that much anyway.

Therefore one thing above any other occupied my mind from seven until twelve when I got my bike, the thought of seeing my big brother Ken.

Once I got my bike I did just that. For five years every weekend and every single holiday I pedalled from Wath to R.A.F. Hemswell in Lincolnshire, a distance of about fifty miles each way to spend all my time with Ken and his family. It was a magic time of my life.

I can't remember ever missing a weekend in five years. In rain, snow or wind I went, and on one occasion when for some reason I couldn't go on my bike, I went by bus and train to Gainsborough on a Friday night, then walked the fourteen miles to Hemswell on my own. There to spend just one day before having to go home again.

I have worked it out that in that five year period I pedalled over 25000 miles to be with my brother. Shall I tell you something, it was worth it, my dream had come true.